Amish
COOKING CLASS
COOKBOOK

WANDA &
BRUNSTETTER

SHILOH RUN PRESS
An Imprint of Barbour Publishing, Inc.

Print ISBN 978-1-68322-466-2

All scripture quotations are taken from the King James Version of the Bible.

Compiled by Janice Thompson.

Cover images: (top) Richard Brunstetter III; (bottom middle) Doyle Yoder, DYP, Inc. Interior images: pages 14, 60, 130, 142, 152, 174, 186 - Doyle Yoder, DYP, Inc.; all other images - Shutterstock

Published by Shiloh Run Press, an imprint of Barbour Publishing, Inc., 1810 Barbour Drive, Uhrichsville, OH 44683, www.shilohrunpress.com

Our mission is to inspire the world with the life-changing message of the Bible.

Member of the
Evangelical Christian
Publishers Association

Printed in China.

INTRODUCTION *and* ACKNOWLEDGMENTS
for the Amish COOKING CLASS COOKBOOK:

When I decided to write the Amish Cooking Class series of novels, I thought about all the delicious meals my husband and I have eaten in many of our Amish friends' homes. I've never met an Amish woman who wasn't a great cook, and Heidi Troyer, the main character in this series, is no exception. My Amish friends have given me many tasty recipes over the years, which I've shared with my own family. One of my favorites is Haystack, and it is included in this wonderful cookbook.

This special recipe collection is a companion to the three books in my Amish Cooking Class series. It contains most of the recipes Heidi taught to a variety of students in each of her classes. In addition, Heidi's students—even the children she taught—have shared some of their favorite recipes for you to try.

A special thanks to Janice Thompson for writing the articles and compiling all the main dishes, desserts, snacks, baked goods, and miscellaneous items that were included in this cookbook. Many of the extra recipes came from women in various Amish communities.

There's an old Pennsylvania Dutch saying: "Kissin' don't last, but good cookin' does." I hope you will enjoy the variety of recipes, as well as the advice from fellow cooks, and articles about Amish life before each section.

Happy Cooking!

Wanda E. Brunstetter

Contents

O taste and see
that the LORD is good:
blessed is the man that
trusteth in him.

Psalm 34:8

Amish Cooking Class

CAST OF CHARACTERS

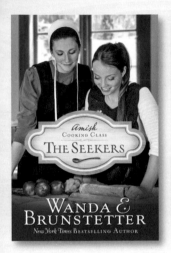
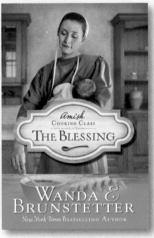
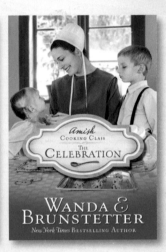

Heidi Troyer: Heidi and her husband have been married eight years, but they don't have children. Looking for something of purpose to fill her days, she decides to start offering cooking classes in her Amish home located in Holmes County, Ohio. Many different people come, and unlikely friendships are formed. Heidi loves to cook and particularly likes to eat the Amish Haystack, German Potato Salad, and Pumpkin Whoopie Pies.

Lyle Troyer: Heidi's husband is an auctioneer. He doesn't attend her classes, but he does offer support wherever he can. Lyle likes to barbecue ribs and anything else one might cook on the grill during warmer weather.

Book 1
THE SEEKERS

— ⁘ —

Charlene Higgins: A teacher of kindergarten, her hobby is photography. Charlene doesn't cook well, and since she's engaged to be married, she took Heidi's class to learn how to cook and impress her in-laws. She enjoys Chinese food and chocolate brownies.

Ron Hensley: He is an ex-marine who served in the Vietnam War. Ron is unemployed and travels around the country in an old motor home. Ron ended up taking the class because he was camped on Heidi and Lyle's property. His favorite foods are ham and eggs.

Kendra Perkins: Currently unemployed and expecting a baby, Kendra's friend gave her the class as a gift, hoping it would cheer Kendra up. Her food cravings are pizza and chocolate ice cream.

Loretta Donnelly: She is widowed and raising two children. Currently unemployed, Loretta enjoys gardening. She took the class to learn more about the Amish way of life. Her favorite foods are fried chicken and chocolate chip cookies.

Eli Miller: A widower, he does woodworking for a living. Eli took Heidi's class because he needed to learn how to cook for himself. He likes pumpkin cinnamon rolls and taffy, which his wife used to make.

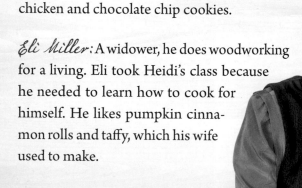

Book 2
THE BLESSING

Lance Freemont: He is a mail carrier who took Heidi's class for something unique and fun to do. Lance enjoys fried potatoes with onions and chocolate cream pie.

Todd Collins: As a food critic for a local newspaper, Todd took Heidi's class to learn more about the types of meals the Amish cook. He likes to try out new recipes, and his favorites foods are filet mignon, eggs Benedict, and crème brulee.

Bill Mason: He is the head janitor at a high school. Bill took the class to impress his hunting buddies with some new meals on their hunting trips. He loves hot dogs with sauerkraut, hunter's stew, and strawberry ice cream.

Nicole Smith: A high school student who helps her dad care for her siblings, Nicole took the class to learn how to cook better. Her favorite foods are pizza, toasted cheese sandwiches, and candy bars.

Lisa Brooks: She owns her own catering business. By taking Heidi's class, Lisa hopes to offer more variety in the meals and desserts she makes for her clients. Lisa personally loves to eat pasta dishes, spinach/strawberry salad, and peanut butter cookies.

Allie Garrett: She is married to a policeman and took the class because her husband gave it to her as a gift. Allie's favorite foods are nachos, enchiladas, and glazed donuts.

Book 3

THE CELEBRATION

Randy Olsen: He is five years old and living with Heidi and Lyle as a foster child. Heidi decided to teach a children's cooking class, thinking it would be fun for Randy and his sister, Marsha, and give them a chance to meet other children. Randy's favorite foods are hot dogs, spaghetti, chicken nuggets, and chocolate chip cookies.

Marsha Olsen: Randy's three-year-old sister, Marsha, is living as a foster child with the Troyers. She likes peanut butter and jelly sandwiches, chicken nuggets, and chocolate ice cream.

Denise McGuire: Denise is a busy real estate broker who makes time to take her daughter to Heidi's cooking class for children. She enjoys fine foods like prime rib, spinach soufflé, and chocolate mousse.

Kassidy McGuire: Kassidy doesn't want to go to a cooking class, but her mother, Denise, insisted it would be something fun to do. Her favorite foods are fried chicken, macaroni and cheese, and strawberry ice cream.

Darren Keller: He is a widower, raising his ten-year-old son, Jeremy. He takes Jeremy to the classes thinking it will be something different and fun for the boy to do during summer vacation. Darren is a fireman and who prefers burgers, pizza, and root beer floats.

Jeremy Keller: He is Darren's son who isn't thrilled about having to attend cooking classes. His favorite foods are pizza, hot dogs, and popcorn with lots of butter.

Ellen Blackburn: As a single mother and busy nurse, Ellen thinks a cooking class could benefit her daughter, Becky. Ellen's choice foods are healthy salads, baked chicken, fish, and many kinds of fruits.

Becky Blackburn: She attends Heidi's cooking class with her mother, Ellen. Her favorite foods are homemade pizza, grape juice, and peach yogurt.

Trent Cooper: The father of Kevin, who is six, and Debbie, who is eight, Trent sells cars for a living. His favorite meal would include sirloin steak, loaded baked potato, and chocolate cake.

Miranda Cooper: She is Kevin and Debbie's mother who works at a local grocery store. Her favorite foods are lasagna, roast with potatoes and carrots, and peach pie.

Kevin Cooper: He is Miranda and Trent's six-year-old son who is pushed into cooking class by his mother. Kevin likes chicken nuggets, pizza, and bananas.

Debbie Cooper: Miranda and Trent's eight-year-old daughter attends Heidi's classes with her brother, Kevin. Her favorite foods are hot dogs, macaroni and cheese, and peanut butter cookies.

Velma Kimball: Velma brings her eight-year-old daughter, Peggy Ann, to the cooking classes, hoping she will make some new friends. Velma does some work for Heidi in order to pay for the classes. Her favorite foods are sauerkraut and pork, scrambled eggs with salsa, and fresh strawberries with milk.

Peggy Ann Kimball: She is eight years old and tends to be a bit shy until she gets to know people. Peggy Ann likes most foods, but especially hot dogs with ketchup.

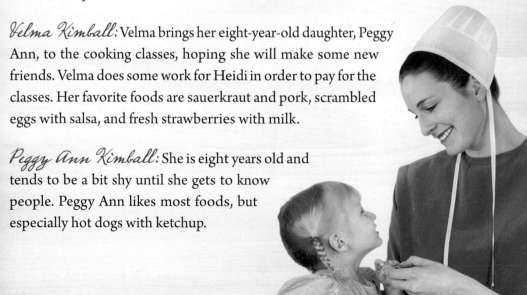

Amish Cooking

Step into the Amish kitchen—a warm and cozy place where the whole family can gather.

Amish families design their kitchens—and meals—to reflect their peaceful, simplistic lifestyle. No crazy, fast-paced living here. Instead of frozen chicken nuggets, you are more likely to find an Amish cook starting with the whole bird. Because she's not racing against the clock to get the kids to that next soccer game or ballet class, you will discover a woman who takes her time and enjoys the details.

While some modern Amish women do use shortcuts at mealtime—and let's face it, what sort of woman doesn't like a good shortcut?—they also value the time it takes to serve good, hearty foods, packed with nutritional value. Many of the Amish still live at least partially off the land, in much the same way our ancestors did. Instead of finding prepackaged produce, you will likely encounter a woman who tends to her garden and feeds her family from the fruits (and vegetables) of her labor.

Simple. Sustainable. These are words that describe Amish cooking styles. And while it might not seem "simple" to go to such lengths, the payoff is in the taste and appearance of the food. A great deal of care and effort goes into each meal. Cooking for the Amish is an act of service, another way to worship the Creator.

This is where the Amish cook excels: She cherishes and serves those she loves. And, while Amish women love to cook, they enjoy family mealtime even more. There's nothing finer than gathering around the family table with husband and children.

Two words propel the Amish cook as she labors for those she loves: service and celebration. She works hard and focuses on the details of each meal. This service-oriented cook delivers hearty meals to her husband and children in order to fill their stomachs after a hard day's work. She also uses food to celebrate life. While other areas of the Amish cook's life are more restrained (clothing, entertainment, etc.), food is not. Here, she can celebrate in style, creating masterpieces for all to enjoy.

No time is this more evident than when the community shows up for an event. It's quite the production as the women combine their efforts to produce a meal no one will soon forget. No fast-food pickups on the way to an Amish event! These ladies spend hours in preparation. Running out of food is not an option. If these ladies think you might be hungry, they feed you. . .and feed you again.

Amish cooks lead with their hearts, and their delicious meals are evidence of that.

Advice from Fellow Cooks

*My mouth shall speak of wisdom;
and the meditation of my heart
shall be of understanding.*

Psalm 49:3

For Tender Roast Beef

Flour and sear the meat first and then add water and vegetables.

Personal-Sized Meat Loaves

Cook meat loaf in a muffin tin and store in the freezer in freezer-safe plastic bags. Note: Meatloaf muffins will cook in approximately half of the usual time.

Fish Tips

Before using fresh fish in any recipe, wash it in cool water and pat completely dry.

The Quickest Way to Peel Potatoes

Place whole potatoes in boiling water. Let them sit for a few minutes and the skins will peel right off.

Keep Potatoes White

To keep your potatoes from turning black after peeling, soak them in cold water. Make sure they are fully covered. You can refrigerate them overnight this way. (Be sure to cover with plastic wrap.)

Presoak Pasta for Fast Cooking

Soak your pasta in water in a sealed bag for a couple of hours or overnight. Drain and boil in fresh water. It will be fully cooked after 1 minute.

Caramelize Onions Quicker

Caramelize onions in a fraction of the time by adding baking soda.

Squash Seeds

Scoop seeds from squash with an ice cream scoop.

Baking Tip

For the best possible outcome, start out with your eggs and butter at room temperature. Ingredients will blend easier and faster.

For Fluffy Cookies

For lighter, fluffier cookies, use vegetable shortening in place of butter.

Salvaging Burned Cookies or Toast

Use a handheld grater or zester to shave the char from slightly burned cookies or toast.

Dress up a Boxed Cake Mix

To make a boxed cake taste homemade, substitute butter for oil and add milk instead of water. Add a teaspoon of vanilla and/or almond extract to white cakes for additional flavor.

Low and Slow Baking

Set oven temperatures lower for bigger cake pans. The cake will have to bake longer, but you won't run the risk of burning the outer edges by the time the middle is done.

Get Air Bubbles out of Cake Batter

To ensure your cakes don't have big air holes, fill the pans with batter, then lift and drop the pans several times until air bubbles rise to the surface and then pop.

Cake Leveler

Need to trim off the top of your cake layers before stacking and filling? Use dental floss in a back and forth motion for a perfectly straight cut.

Frosting Bag Tip

Need to fill a frosting bag? Place it in a tall cup and fold the edges down.

Turn Cake Mix into Brownies

Need to make brownies in a hurry but don't have the ingredients? Use a chocolate cake mix instead. Add only 2 eggs and ⅓ cup oil (or butter). Scoop batter into greased pan and bake. (Additional things to add to batter: pecans/walnuts, chocolate chips, white chocolate chips, etc.)

Muffin Tin Cookie Bowls

Want to make cookie bowls for your next ice cream sundae? Flip a muffin tin upside down and mold cookie dough over the bottom of each cup. Bake at 350 degrees for 20 minutes.

Pie Crust

For the flakiest possible crust, use ice-cold water. Add a pinch of salt for better taste.

Make Your Own Powdered Sugar

Need powdered sugar for a recipe but don't have any on hand? No problem. Just take a scoop of granulated sugar and put it into your spice grinder or food processor. It will pulverize and turn into fluffy white powdered sugar, right before your very eyes.

Corn Syrup Substitute

Out of light corn syrup? Just combine 1 cup sugar with ¼ cup water.

Egg Hacks

To keep eggs from cracking while boiling, add either vinegar or salt. To easily peel a hard-boiled egg, allow it to cool completely and then place it in a drinking glass and shake back and forth. The shell should come right off.

DIY Buttermilk

To make your own buttermilk, combine ¾ cup Greek yogurt with ¼ cup water and mix well.

Measuring Tip

Some recipes will call for a pinch or a dash of salt or other ingredient. Experienced cooks get a feel for what those mean, but a beginning cook can use this general reference:

Tad = ¼ teaspoon
Dash = ⅛ teaspoon
Pinch = $\frac{1}{16}$ teaspoon
Smidgen = $\frac{1}{32}$ teaspoon

Measuring Flour

Flour packs down, so your method of measuring can have an effect on how much you actually get and change the outcome of your recipe. To start, use a spoon to stir the flour in your storage container that has settled together. Then use the spoon to gently fill your measuring cup. Use a flat edge like a knife to level off the top of the cup's contents back into the flour bin. If the recipe calls for sifted flour, measure out the listed amount, then sift it. If you don't have a flour sifter, you can put the flour into a strainer and shake it into your mixing bowl. Or, you can also sift or fluff your flour with a whisk or fork if necessary.

Dehydration

Want to dehydrate veggies or meats but don't own one of those fancy dehydrators? Use your oven instead. Cut food into ¼-inch slices and place on lined baking sheet. Set your oven on the lowest possible setting for 6 to 8 hours.

Freeze Your Sauces

Wondering what to do with that leftover pasta sauce? Pour it into an ice cube tray, cover, and freeze for later use.

Easy Access Bananas

For easier access, open bananas from the bottom of the banana instead of the stem. (This is how monkeys open their bananas, after all.)

Fruit Saver

Wondering what to do with those bananas before they turn black? Don't think you can eat all those grapes before they spoil? Freeze them for later use. (Note: Peel and cube bananas before freezing.)

Basic Recipes

How to Boil Eggs

Place eggs in pot and cover with cold water. Bring water to boil over high heat. When water reaches a hard boil, cover pot with lid and turn off heat. Let eggs cook for 8 to 10 minutes for soft yolk or 12 to 15 minutes for harder yolk. Drain off hot water and move eggs to a bowl of water and ice. Chill for 5 minutes. Drain. Let eggs reach room temperature, then peel.

How to Boil Potatoes

When making a potato salad or some potato casseroles, you first need to boil your potatoes. Choose an all-purpose potato with low starch like red, white, or Yukon Gold. Wash and peel. Cut to uniform size if needed—about 2 inches. Place potatoes in a pot and cover with cold water. Add a generous amount of salt—1 tablespoon to a large pot. Bring water to a rolling boil. Cook 8 to 10 minutes until a fork easily pierces into the potatoes. Drain. If your recipe calls for grating the cooked potato, cook for a shorter time.

How to Cook Rice

For most medium to long grain rice, use a 1:2 ratio of 1 cup rice to 2 cups water. Plan ½ cup uncooked rice per person. In a heavy saucepan, bring water to rolling boil. Add ½ teaspoon salt per cup of rice, then add rice. Put on lid and don't remove during cooking so the steam is not released. Turn heat to lowest setting. Cook about 20 minutes for white rice and 30 minutes for brown rice. After time, remove lid and fluff rice with a fork. Rice is done when tender. There may be a bit of water remaining in the pot to drain off. Rice may also be a bit sticky, but that is okay. You just don't want to overcook it until it is gummy.

How to Boil Chicken

Place chicken in a pot and cover with water. Add salt. Bring to a boil, cover, and cook over medium heat. Boneless chicken breasts should cook in 15 minutes. A whole bone-in chicken will take 45 to 60 minutes. Remove from water. Retain water to use as chicken broth. Cool chicken and remove any bones. (Bones can be cooked for bone broth.) Chop or shred chicken as called for in recipes.

How to Cook Bone Broth

Beef bones can be bought from the butcher or in grocery stores. Raw bones would benefit from being roasted in the oven at 350 degrees for 30 minutes before making broth. For poultry broth, save the bones from your chicken or turkey meals. Some meat on the bones is fine, but discard the skin. You can freeze bones until you have saved enough for a pot of broth. Place bones in a large pot or Crock-Pot and cover with water. Add 1 to 2 tablespoons of apple cider vinegar to help release the minerals from the bones. You can also add some vegetables like onion, carrot, and celery. Bring to a boil; cook over low heat for about 1 hour for poultry to 2 or more hours for beef. Occasionally skim any foam from the top of the broth. Strain and use.

How to Make a White Sauce

A white sauce is a basic component to many cream soups, casseroles, gravies, or pasta sauces. In a saucepan over medium heat, melt 2 tablespoons of butter. Add 2 tablespoons of flour and cook until incorporated. Slowly pour in 1 cup of milk, stirring or whisking constantly as it cooks and thickens.

How to Roast Vegetables

Set oven to 425 degrees. Chop vegetables. Firm vegetables like cauliflower, broccoli, potatoes, and carrots will take longer to cook than soft vegetables like summer squash, mushrooms, onion, and tomatoes, so either cut your firm vegetables smaller or add the soft vegetables later in the roasting process. Lightly toss vegetables in olive oil, salt, and pepper. Spread in a single layer on a baking sheet. Bake 30 to 40 minutes until tender.

How to Whip Cream

Pour cold heavy whipping cream into a deep bowl. Whisk by hand or use an electric mixture until peaks begin to form as cream stiffens. Add a little sugar and a dash of vanilla. Serve chilled.

RECIPES FOR BEVERAGES

~~~

*Whether therefore ye eat,
or drink, or whatsoever ye do,
do all to the glory of God.*

1 CORINTHIANS 10:31

~~~

Almond Milk

1 cup raw almonds
2 cups water, plus additional water
   for soaking

Honey to taste

Place almonds in bowl and cover with water. Cover and let stand overnight. Drain and rinse under cool water. Discard water. Put mushy almonds and 2 cups water into blender. Pulse for 2 minutes to break up almonds, then blend thoroughly for 2 minutes. Strain through cheesecloth. Press all almond milk from meal. If sweetener is desired, add honey. Refrigerate.

Ellen Blackburn

*Ellen loves healthy food options and likes that
she can make a dairy-free milk from scratch.*

Bavarian Mint Coffee

⅓ cup nondairy powdered
   coffee creamer
⅓ cup sugar

⅓ cup instant coffee
2 tablespoons cocoa
6 hard peppermint candies, crushed

In small bowl, combine creamer, sugar, instant coffee, and cocoa. Set aside. Crush candies to fine powder and combine with dry mixture. Store in airtight container. Use 2 to 2½ teaspoons per cup of boiling water.

Todd Collins

*Todd has a taste for the finer things, which is why he
particularly enjoys this recipe for Bavarian Mint Coffee.*

Chocolate Coffee Smoothies

3 cups ice cubes or frozen milk cubes
1 cup milk
½ cup maple syrup

2 teaspoons instant coffee
1 tablespoon chocolate syrup
½ teaspoon vanilla

Mix everything together in blender until smooth.

Susan Lehman, *Robinson, IL*

EGGNOG

4 large farm-fresh eggs
1/3 cup sugar
1/8 teaspoon nutmeg
4 tablespoons lemon juice

1/8 teaspoon salt
4 cups milk
1/2 cup heavy whipping cream

Beat eggs until thick. Whisk in sugar, nutmeg, lemon juice, and salt. Add milk and cream. Beat with mixer until eggnog is foamy/frothy. Serve with ice.

Velma Kimball

Velma's not just crazy about eggs; she's also pretty crazy about this wonderful eggnog recipe!

Orange Julius

1 cup milk

2 teaspoons vanilla

1 (6 ounce) can frozen orange juice
   concentrate

½ cup sugar

1½ cups ice cubes

Combine milk and vanilla in blender. Add orange juice concentrate. Blend until fully incorporated. Add sugar and ice cubes. Blend until cubes are crushed. Mixture will thicken. You can add additional water if results are too thick for your taste.

Kendra Perkins
Kendra's not-so-secret craving
during pregnancy? Orange Julius!

GRAPE JUICE TO CAN

2 cups grapes   ½ cup sugar

Put grapes into sterilized canning jar and add sugar. Fill to top with boiling water. Seal. Process in water bath for 10 minutes. The following day, remove metal lid bands and label with date and contents. Let grape juice stand for 3 to 4 weeks before using. Strain juice from grapes.

Loretta Donnelly

This was one of Loretta's first canning projects after joining the Amish church. Simple, but tasty.

MAPLE HOT CHOCOLATE

2 tablespoons unsweetened cocoa   ¼ cup maple syrup
⅛ teaspoon salt   4 cups milk
¼ cup water   1 teaspoon vanilla

Whisk together cocoa, salt, water, and syrup in saucepan. Gradually whisk in milk. Bring to a simmer over medium heat. Remove from heat; stir in vanilla.

Denise McGuire

Denise is crazy about all things chocolate and can't get enough of this new twist on an old favorite.

ROOT BEER

2 cups sugar   3 teaspoons root beer extract
¾ teaspoon yeast   1 gallon warm water

Combine ingredients and divide into bottles with lids. Let stand in warm place overnight. Put in refrigerator. Will get stronger the longer you keep it.

MIRIAM HERSHBERGER, *Apple Creek, OH*

SPICED CRANBERRY PUNCH

2 quarts cranberry juice
2¾ cups water
1¼ cups sugar
16 whole cloves

1 teaspoon cinnamon
½ teaspoon nutmeg
⅔ cup orange juice
½ cup lemon juice

Combine cranberry juice, water, and sugar in large saucepan and bring to a boil over medium heat. Place cloves in cheesecloth and tie up. Add cinnamon, nutmeg, and cheesecloth with cloves to pan. Lower heat and simmer uncovered for 20 minutes. Discard spice bag, then stir in orange and lemon juice; heat. Serve warm.

WEDDING PUNCH

6 packages Tropical Punch
   Kool-Aid
1 large can/bottle pineapple juice
1 large can/bottle grapefruit juice
2 (12 ounce) cans frozen
   lemonade mix

5 cups sugar
12 quarts water
1 quart ginger ale, frozen just to
   the slushy stage

Combine all ingredients except ginger ale. Add ginger ale prior to serving.

Loretta Donnelly and Eli Miller
*Loretta and Eli enjoyed serving this
punch to their wedding guests.*

The Amish Kitchen

Many have wondered what an Amish kitchen looks like. If Amish women don't have ready access to electricity, how do they cook? Are they limited as to what they can make, and how?

It might surprise some to learn that many Amish cooks have fully equipped kitchens that include stoves fueled with propane gas or kerosene oil for cooking, gas-run refrigerators, as well as mixers and other such devices that run on air power. Not all Amish permit such luxuries, but many do.

The Amish kitchen is filled with practical, homey items. You won't often find high-end decor there, but you will find sturdy tables, solid cabinets, and a well-stocked pantry. You might not see over-the-top light fixtures, but you will often notice large windows and skylights for natural lighting.

So, how do the Amish store all that food? Most Amish have refrigerators and some have freezers, but many still cool their foods in iceboxes, basements, or springhouses. Fruits and vegetables are canned, along with many of their meats, so you will find ample food items. Rural Amish often own their own milk cows. If so, you will find homemade cheeses, yogurts, and even ice creams.

How are these foods served? If you are lucky enough to visit an Amish home, you might find yourself eating on lovely ceramic plates, handcrafted by a local artisan. Even the sugar bowls, creamers, and other dishes are often made in the area—shaped and fired in local kilns. These handcrafted beauties are often painted in varying shades with exquisite roses and other flowers. Basket weaving is another art form that often makes its way into the Amish kitchen. You can find woven silverware baskets, serving trays, and napkin baskets in many homes.

Of course, Amish sects vary, as do their customs. In many Old-Order homes, you will find manual hand-cranked stand mixers, along with stove-top waffle irons and coffee percolators. You'll likely hear the whistle of the teakettle and observe cast-iron skillets and pots hanging from hooks, ready for use.

In short, the Amish kitchen is well equipped and ready to put out the heartiest food for a hungry family and guests.

Recipes for Breads and Rolls

*And Jesus said unto them,
I am the bread of life: he that cometh
to me shall never hunger; and he that
believeth on me shall never thirst.*

John 6:35

Amish Dinner Rolls

2 large eggs
⅓ cup sugar
1½ teaspoons salt
6 tablespoons butter, softened to room
temperature

1 cup mashed cooked potato
2½ teaspoons instant yeast
¾ cup lukewarm water (same water
potatoes were boiled in)
4¼ to 5¼ cups flour

Add all ingredients, except flour, to large mixing bowl. Add 3 cups flour and mix. Add remaining flour, a little at a time, until soft dough forms. Move dough to second bowl that has been lightly greased. Cover with plastic wrap and let sit until dough's size doubles. (This should take approximately 1½ hours.) Carefully deflate dough and put on floured surface. Begin to knead dough with additional flour until it forms a soft, workable texture. Divide into 24 balls and place in lightly greased 9x13-inch pan. Cover pan with lightly greased plastic wrap and allow rolls to rise for an additional 1½ to 2 hours, until dough becomes puffy. Preheat oven to 350 degrees and bake rolls for about 20 to 25 minutes, until they reach a beautiful golden brown. Brush with butter and enjoy!

AMISH CINNAMON BREAD

1 cup butter, softened
2 cups sugar
2 eggs

2 cups buttermilk (or 2 cups milk plus 2
    tablespoons vinegar or lemon juice)
4 cups flour, divided
2 teaspoons baking soda

CINNAMON-SUGAR MIXTURE:

⅔ cup sugar

2 teaspoons cinnamon

Cream butter; add sugar and eggs, one at a time. Add milk, then add 2 cups flour. Mix. Add remaining flour and baking soda. Using two greased loaf pans, put one-quarter of batter into each. In separate bowl, combine ⅔ cup sugar and cinnamon. Sprinkle three-quarters of cinnamon-sugar mixture on top of batter in each loaf pan. Top off with remaining batter, then sprinkle with remaining cinnamon-sugar. Swirl with knife. Bake at 350 degrees for 45 to 50 minutes. Cool before removing from pan.

Bill Mason

*Bill loves to make a batch of this Amish Cinnamon
Bread before heading out to the deer stand.
Perfect for a chilly morning.*

APRICOT DATE NUT LOAF

1¾ cups water
¾ cup pitted dates, chopped
¾ cup dried apricots, chopped
2 teaspoons baking soda
1½ cups sugar

1 stick butter
2 eggs, beaten
2½ cups flour
1 cup chopped pecans

Start by boiling water. Place dates and apricots into mixing bowl and add baking soda, sugar, and butter. Pour boiling water over other ingredients and let stand until butter has melted and mixture has cooled. Add beaten eggs, along with flour and pecans. Pour into two loaf pans lined with greased parchment paper. Bake at 350 degrees for 1 hour or until done.

Amish Friendship Bread

1 cup starter

3 eggs

1 cup oil

½ cup milk

½ teaspoon vanilla

2 cups flour

1 cup sugar

2 teaspoons cinnamon

1½ teaspoons baking powder

½ teaspoon salt

½ teaspoon baking soda

1 to 2 small boxes instant pudding (any flavor)

1 cup nuts, chopped (optional)

1 cup raisins (optional)

½ cup sugar

½ teaspoon cinnamon

Preheat oven to 325 degrees. Grease and flour two large loaf pans. Mix starter, eggs, oil, milk, and vanilla. In separate bowl, mix flour, 1 cup sugar, 2 teaspoons cinnamon, baking powder, salt, baking soda, pudding mix, and nuts and/or raisins, if desired. Add to liquid mixture and stir thoroughly. Mix ½ cup sugar and ½ teaspoon cinnamon and dust greased pans lightly. Pour batter evenly into pans and sprinkle remaining cinnamon-sugar mixture on top. Bake for 1 hour or until toothpick inserted in center of bread comes out clean.

OPTIONS:

- Use 2 boxes pudding mix. Change flavor of pudding mix.
- Add up to 2 cups dried fruit or baking chips (note: Heavier add-ins may sink to bottom).
- Decrease fat by substituting ½ cup oil and ½ cup applesauce for 1 cup oil in recipe.
- Decrease eggs by using 2 eggs and ¼ cup mashed banana.
- Use large Bundt pan rather than two loaf pans.

RECIPE FOR STARTER:

¼ cup warm water

1 (¼ ounce) packet yeast

1½ cups plus 1 tablespoon sugar

3 cups milk

3 cups flour

DAY 1: Put warm water in bowl; add yeast. Sprinkle 1 tablespoon sugar over it and let stand in warm place (about 10 minutes). Mix ½ cup sugar, 1 cup milk, 1 cup flour, and yeast mixture. Stir with wooden spoon. Do not use metal spoon as it will retard the yeast's growth. Cover loosely and let stand at room temperature overnight.

DAYS 2–4: Stir starter each day with wooden spoon. Cover loosely again.

DAY 5: Stir in ½ cup sugar, 1 cup milk, and 1 cup flour. Mix well. Cover loosely.

DAYS 6–9: Stir well each day and cover loosely.

DAY 10: Stir in ½ cup sugar, 1 cup milk, and 1 cup flour. It's now ready to use to make bread. Remove 1 cup to make your first bread. Give 1 cup each to two friends, along with recipe for starter and your favorite Amish bread. Store remaining starter in container in refrigerator (or freeze) to make future bread.

Heidi Troyer

Friendship Bread is a staple in Heidi and Lyle's home. She considers it part of her ministry because it opens doors to new friendships and gives her plenty of opportunity to share with others in her community.

ANGEL BISCUITS

3 cups flour
3 tablespoons baking powder
1 teaspoon angel cream (replacement
    for cream of tartar)

1 teaspoon salt
2 eggs, beaten
¾ cup oil
2 cups milk

In large bowl, mix together flour, baking powder, angel cream, and salt. Add eggs, oil, and milk. Mix well. Pour into greased jelly roll pan and bake at 350 degrees for 25 minutes until golden brown. Very good served with chicken or sausage gravy.

KAREN MILLER, *Monroe, WI*

APPLE CORN BREAD

¾ cup cornmeal
¾ cup spelt or whole wheat flour
3 teaspoons baking powder
¼ teaspoon cloves
1 teaspoon cinnamon
¾ teaspoon salt

1 egg, beaten
1 teaspoon vanilla
¾ cup buttermilk
2 tablespoons oil or melted butter
1 tablespoon honey
2 cups diced apples

Sift dry ingredients together in bowl. Add egg, vanilla, and buttermilk. Blend well. Add oil, honey, and apples. Mix thoroughly. Pour into greased 9-inch square pan. Bake at 350 degrees for 25 minutes.

Heidi Troyer

BANANA BREAD

2 cups mashed bananas
4 eggs
1 cup oil
2 teaspoons vanilla
⅔ cup buttermilk

3½ cups flour
3 cups sugar
2 teaspoons baking soda
1 teaspoon salt

Mix all ingredients well. Pour into two greased and floured loaf pans. Bake at 300 degrees for 1 hour or until toothpick comes out clean.

KATIE YODER, *Fultonville, NY*

Garlic Loaf

3 tablespoons butter, divided
2 cans refrigerated biscuits
2 cloves garlic, minced

3 tablespoons grated Parmesan
cheese

Melt 1 tablespoon of butter and pour in bottom of loaf pan. Lay one log of biscuits on each side of pan. Fan out biscuits and drizzle remaining butter melted with garlic over the top, in between, and around the sides. Scatter cheese over top and in between biscuits. Bake at 350 degrees for 30 minutes, or until center is solid. Serve warm, pulling apart the sections.

Charlene Higgins
So easy and so good!

Bran Muffins

5 cups flour, sifted
3 cups sugar
12 ounces bran cereal
5 teaspoons baking soda
2 teaspoons salt

1 teaspoon cinnamon
½ teaspoon allspice
4 eggs, beaten
1 quart buttermilk
1 cup oil

Mix dry ingredients, then add eggs, buttermilk, and oil. Pour into lined muffin tins and bake at 400 degrees for 15 to 20 minutes.

Johnnycakes

1¼ cups milk	2 tablespoons sugar
1 tablespoon butter	1 teaspoon baking powder
½ cup flour	1 teaspoon salt
1 cup cornmeal	1 egg, lightly beaten

Bring milk and butter to a simmer. In separate bowl, combine flour, cornmeal, sugar, baking powder, and salt. Whisk. Add heated milk to dry ingredients and blend, then whisk in beaten egg. Fry on greased griddle or skillet until golden brown on both sides. Serve hot with butter and syrup as for pancakes, or serve as bread with butter. Increase or decrease amount of sugar, depending on your preference.

Nichole Smith

Nichole is always looking for quick, easy recipes. She found a winner with these yummy Johnnycakes, which her younger siblings love.

Sweet Potato Biscuits

1¼ cups flour	¾ cup mashed cooked sweet potato
2 heaping tablespoons sugar	¼ cup butter
4 teaspoons baking powder	2 to 4 tablespoons milk (depending on moisture of potatoes)
½ teaspoon salt	2 to 3 tablespoons melted butter

Sift together flour, sugar, baking powder, and salt. In separate bowl, combine sweet potato and butter. Add flour mixture until you end up with soft dough. Add milk 1 tablespoon at a time and continue to cut in. Turn dough out onto floured board and toss lightly until outside of dough looks smooth. Roll dough out to ½-inch thick and cut with biscuit cutter. Place biscuits on greased pan and coat tops with melted butter. Bake for about 15 minutes at 450 degrees.

Peggy Ann Kimball

Peggy Ann enjoyed learning to make these biscuits with her mom.

No Knead Whole Wheat Bread

1 tablespoon yeast
1¼ cups warm water
2 tablespoons butter, melted
1 teaspoon salt

1½ cups whole wheat flour
1½ cups all-purpose flour
1 egg

Mix all ingredients and set aside to rise until doubled in size—about 30 minutes. Stir dough 30 strokes with spoon. Pour batter into greased loaf pan. Cover and let rise in warm place. Bake at 350 degrees for 30 minutes.

ANNA YODER, *Fairchild, WI*

Pecan Cherry Bread

½ cup butter, softened
¾ cup sugar
2 eggs
2 cups flour
1 teaspoon baking soda
½ teaspoon salt

1 cup buttermilk
1 cup chopped pecans
1 (10 ounce) jar maraschino cherries,
    drained and chopped
1 teaspoon vanilla

Cream butter, then add sugar until thoroughly incorporated. Add eggs, one at a time, stirring well after each. In separate bowl, combine flour, baking soda, and salt. Add dry ingredients to butter and egg mixture alternately with buttermilk. Stir in pecans, cherries, and vanilla. Pour into greased and floured loaf pan. Bake at 350 degrees for 65 to 75 minutes.

Sourdough Bread

STARTER:

½ cup sugar

⅓ cup instant potatoes

⅓ cup instant yeast

2 cups warm water

Mix well. Loosely cover and let sit at room temperature at least 8 hours or overnight.

BREAD DOUGH:

⅔ cup sugar

2 tablespoons instant yeast

2 tablespoons salt

3 cups warm water

2 cups starter

1 cup oil

½ cup Do-Cel dough conditioner (optional)*

½ cup water if using conditioner (optional)*

13 to 15 cups flour

In large bowl, dissolve sugar, yeast, and salt in warm water. Add remaining ingredients, except flour; mix well. Add flour a little at a time until you have good dough consistency. Let rise until doubled, then shape into loaves and put into loaf pans. Prick loaves with fork and let rise. Bake at 350 degrees for 50 to 60 minutes until golden brown.

*Always add equal parts Do-Cel and extra water.

RHONDA RAPP, *Crofton, KY*

SPICED APPLE MUFFINS

1 egg	4 teaspoons baking powder
1 cup milk	½ teaspoon salt
4 tablespoons melted butter	½ teaspoon cinnamon
2 cups flour	1 cup finely chopped apples
½ cup sugar	

TOPPING:

2 tablespoons sugar	½ teaspoon cinnamon

Combine wet ingredients with dry, then add apples. Spoon batter into lined muffin tin. Combine 2 tablespoons sugar and ½ teaspoon cinnamon and sprinkle on top of muffins. Bake for 15 to 20 minutes at 400 degrees. For additional flavor, add raisins or pecans.

SURPRISE MUFFINS

1 egg	¼ cup sugar
1 cup milk	3 teaspoons baking powder
¼ cup oil	1 teaspoon salt
2 cups flour	Strawberry or blueberry jam

Grease the bottom of muffin cups or use paper baking cups. In a medium-sized mixing bowl, beat egg with a fork. Stir in milk and oil. Blend flour and other dry ingredients until mixture is moistened. Batter may be a bit lumpy. Do not over mix. Fill muffin cups half full of batter. Drop a scant teaspoonful of jam in the center of batter in each muffin cup. Add more batter to fill the cup so it is ⅔ full. Bake at 400 degrees for 20 to 25 minutes or until golden brown. Muffins will have gently rounded and pebbled tops. Loosen immediately and remove with a spatula. Serve warm or cold. Makes 12 medium muffins.

Heidi Trozer

Kids enjoy discovering the jelly inside the muffin.

Zucchini Bread

1 cup oil	1 teaspoon baking soda
3 eggs	1 teaspoon baking powder
2 cups sugar	1 teaspoon cinnamon
2 cups shredded zucchini	½ cup milk
3 cups flour	¾ cup chopped nuts or raisins
1 teaspoon salt	

In bowl, mix together oil, eggs, sugar, and zucchini. Sift together flour, salt, baking soda, baking powder, and cinnamon, then add to first mixture. Add milk and mix. Fold in nuts or raisins. Bake in two greased loaf pans at 350 degrees for 1 hour.

EDNA IRENE MILLER, *Arthur, IL*

Amish Mornings

In the Amish community, getting off to a good start is critical. The first hour of the day sets the tone for the hours that follow. In most rural homes, the parents rise early, some as early as 4:30 or 5:00 a.m. With so much work to be done, they need the extra time to themselves without the little ones underfoot. Discipline is key. So is the daily routine.

Rising before the sun means they have to light their way with kerosene or battery lamps. Fathers and older sons often dress for outdoor work—milking the cows, for instance, and tending the other animals—while the Amish mother heads to the kitchen to prepare breakfast for the family. You won't see her driving through a coffee shop for a high-end cup of coffee. Instead, you'll likely find her adding grounds to the old-fashioned drip pot. Afterward, there are plenty of other tasks: packing lunches for the husband and schoolchildren and prepping the bread dough for the day.

As she works in the quiet of the morning, there is time to spend with the Lord in prayer and to plan meals for the rest of the day. But, before she knows it, it's time to wake the younger children, who need a hearty breakfast before heading off to school at the local one-room schoolhouse.

Faces and hands are washed, hair arranged, and bonnets donned, along with the sturdy clothing all Amish children are accustomed to. Afterward, the children help their mother set the table for breakfast.

When Father re-enters the house, fresh from his morning routine, it's time to consume their first meal of the day. Whether meat will be consumed during the breakfast meal depends on the sect of Amish. If Old-Order rules are in play, keeping meat in cold storage is a challenge, so breakfasts will be heavy on breads, potatoes, and eggs. The Amish wife/mother knows this meal is important, so she fills those tummies with everything her loved ones will need to get through the morning.

Before a bite is taken, the family prays together—though most offer silent prayers, both prior to and after the meal. No cell phones beeping in this house. No TV blaring in the background. Children visit with their parents and make their plans for the day. After the meal, they carry their dishes to the sink. Even the littlest ones help out, as they are able, before heading off to school for the day.

When the Amish housewife finally finds herself alone, she tends to her morning chores, both inside and out. If she has a garden, she works to keep it going. If the interior of her home needs tending to, she takes care of it right away. You won't find many messy kitchens in Amish households. Keeping a clean house is part of the daily discipline, so dishes, sweeping, mopping, and laundry will be high on the morning to-do list.

With so much work to do, Amish mothers probably long for a midmorning nap, but there is always a new chore waiting. Most of these ladies are up for the challenge. They have been taught from a young age the value of hard work, and their dedication to family gives them the strength they need to face each new day.

RECIPES FOR BREAKFAST FOODS

It is of the LORD's mercies that we are not consumed, because his compassions fail not. They are new every morning: great is thy faithfulness.

LAMENTATIONS 3:22–23

Amish Country Breakfast

14 slices whole wheat bread

2½ cups cubed ham

1 pound mozzarella cheese, shredded

1 pound cheddar cheese, shredded

6 eggs

3 cups milk

Topping:

½ cup butter, melted

3 cups cornflakes (do not crush)

Grease 9x13-inch baking pan and layer half the bread, ham, and cheeses. Repeat layers. Beat eggs in mixing bowl, add milk, and pour over layers in pan. Refrigerate overnight. Next morning, preheat oven to 375 degrees. Mix butter and cornflakes. Spread mixture over other ingredients in pan. Cover loosely with foil and bake for 45 minutes.

Heidi Troyer

Heidi's husband, Lyle, works harder than anyone she knows, so a great breakfast is key to starting the day. This tasty casserole hits the spot.

Baked Oatmeal

2 eggs, beaten
1 cup sugar or equivalent substitute
  sweetener
½ cup butter, melted

3 cups oats
1 cup milk
2 teaspoons baking powder
1 pinch salt

Combine eggs, sugar, and butter in 2-quart baking dish. Add oats, milk, baking powder, and salt. Stir until well blended. Bake at 350 degrees for 30 minutes. May be served plain or with milk or whipped cream.

Heidi Troyer
Heidi particularly enjoyed teaching her students
to make this tasty breakfast dish.

Blueberry Pancake Pizza

3 cups prepared pancake batter
1 (21 ounce) can blueberry pie filling
1 dozen eggs

6 cups sausage gravy
1 cup shredded cheese
1 pound bacon, fried and crumbled

Heat oven to 400 degrees. Pour pancake batter into greased and floured 9x13-inch pan. Bake 15 minutes or until done. Cool slightly. Spread with pie filling. Scramble eggs in frying pan. Over pie filling, layer eggs, gravy, cheese, and bacon. Serve with or without maple syrup.

KATIE ZOOK, *Apple Creek, OH*

Night-Before Casserole

4 slices bread, cubed
1 pound sausage, browned
1 cup shredded cheese

6 eggs
2 cups milk

Place bread in bottom of 9x11-inch pan. Place sausage over bread. Top with cheese. Beat eggs and add milk. Pour over casserole. Refrigerate overnight. Bake at 350 degrees for 45 minutes.

ANNA MILLER, *Millersburg, OH*

Cinnamon Pecan Oatmeal

1¼ cups old-fashioned oats
¼ cup pecans, roasted
2 tablespoons brown sugar

2 teaspoons cinnamon
1 pinch salt

Prepare oats according to package directions. Stir in pecans, brown sugar, cinnamon, and salt. Serve with fresh blackberries or additional pecans. It's that simple!

Cheesy Amish Breakfast Casserole

1 pound bacon, diced
1 sweet onion, chopped
4 cups frozen shredded hash brown
    potatoes, thawed

9 eggs, lightly beaten
2 cups shredded cheddar cheese
1½ cups small curd cottage cheese
1¼ cups shredded Swiss cheese

Cook bacon and onion together over medium heat until bacon is evenly browned. Drain. Transfer to large bowl. Stir in all additional ingredients, then pour mixture into greased 9x13-inch baking dish. Bake at 350 degrees for 45 to 50 minutes until eggs are set and cheese is melted.

Allie Garrett

Allie wants cooks everywhere to know that this recipe has her children's stamp of approval. It's her go-to breakfast recipe.

French Toast Casserole

1 cup maple syrup
10 to 16 slices bread
5 eggs

1 teaspoon vanilla
1½ cups milk
¼ teaspoon salt

Pour maple syrup into 9x13-inch pan, coating bottom. Lay bread slices on top. Mix eggs, vanilla, milk, and salt; pour over bread. Refrigerate overnight. Bake covered at 350 degrees for 40 to 45 minutes.

Ruth Ann Yoder, *Salisbury, PA*

FRUIT-FILLED COFFEE CAKE

3 eggs
1½ cups sugar
¾ cup oil
¼ cup orange juice
1 teaspoon vanilla
3 cups flour

3 teaspoons baking powder
1 (21 ounce) can cherry pie filling (or
   your favorite pie filling)
3 tablespoons sugar
1 teaspoon cinnamon

Cream eggs, 1½ cups sugar, oil, juice, and vanilla. Add flour and baking powder; mix well. Pour half of batter into greased 9x13-inch baking dish. Spread pie filling over batter. In small bowl, mix 3 tablespoons sugar and cinnamon; sprinkle 1 teaspoon of mixture over pie filling. Spoon remaining batter over pie filling. Sprinkle with remaining cinnamon-sugar mixture. Bake at 350 degrees for 15 minutes, then reduce heat to 300 degrees and bake an additional 60 minutes.

Nut Crescents

1 cup butter or margarine, softened
½ cup powdered sugar
2 teaspoons vanilla
¼ teaspoon salt

1 cup chopped walnuts, pecans, or almonds
1¾ cups flour

Cream butter. Add powdered sugar, vanilla, and salt and beat until light. Stir in nuts and flour until well blended. Wrap dough in waxed paper and chill well. Divide dough into 8 equal pieces. Shape into thin rolls about ½ inch in diameter. Cut in 2-inch pieces, taper off ends, and shape in crescents. Put on ungreased baking sheet and bake at 300 degrees for 18 to 20 minutes. Sift powdered sugar over top when cooled.

Hootenanny Bread/Pancake

6 eggs
1 cup milk
½ teaspoon salt
1 cup flour
1 stick butter, melted

½ cup sliced strawberries
½ cup blueberries
½ cup raspberries
Powdered sugar

In blender, combine eggs, milk, and salt; blend until frothy. Slowly add flour, mixing until well blended. Pour melted butter into 9x13-inch baking dish, then add egg mixture. Bake at 425 degrees for 25 to 30 minutes or until golden brown. Top with berries and sprinkle with powdered sugar. Slice and serve immediately.

Ron Hensley

Ron never dreamed he'd one day cook up a meal like this, but after taking Heidi's class, he's flipping over these hearty pancakes.

Pancake Mix

8 cups quick oats
8 cups whole wheat flour
8 cups all-purpose flour
¾ cup brown sugar
¾ cup baking powder
2 tablespoons salt
¾ cup butter, melted

Mix all ingredients well and store in airtight container. May use more whole wheat flour if preferred. You may omit butter if you add small amount to batter before cooking.

To use:

4 cups mix
2 eggs, beaten
Milk

In bowl or pitcher, combine mix, eggs, and enough milk to thin to preferred consistency. Fry circles of battle on hot griddle until lightly browned on both sides. Serve with maple syrup.

MATTIE WEAVER, *Stanwood, MI*

Special Request Breakfast Casserole

30 saltine crackers
6 eggs, beaten
6 slices bacon, cooked and crumbled
2 cups milk
2 cups shredded cheddar cheese
¼ cup butter or margarine, melted

Crumble crackers into 8x8-inch baking dish (double recipe to fit 9x13-inch pan). Combine remaining ingredients and pour over crackers. Cover and chill overnight. Remove from refrigerator 30 minutes before baking uncovered at 325 degrees for 45 minutes. Let stand 5 minutes before cutting and serving.

MARY ELLEN WENGERD, *Campbellsville, KY*

Sausage Gravy

1 pound breakfast sausage
⅓ cup flour
3 to 4 cups whole milk
½ teaspoon seasoned salt

2 teaspoons freshly ground black pepper, more to taste
Biscuits, warmed, for serving

Add small pieces of raw sausage to bottom of skillet in thin layer. Brown the sausage over medium-high heat until done. Reduce heat to medium-low. Sprinkle in half of flour. Allow sausage to soak up flour, then add more, little by little. Cook for another minute or so, then pour in milk, stirring constantly. Cook gravy until it thickens, stirring often. Add seasoning and continue cooking until it reaches desired consistency. Adjust seasoning and milk to your liking. Spoon sausage gravy over warm biscuits and serve immediately.

Allie Barrett

*Another quick and easy meal that Allie loves.
She's a mom on the go, after all.*

Syrupy Baked Pancakes and Eggs

1 cup water
⅓ stick butter
¾ cup chicken or beef broth
½ teaspoon stevia powder
1 to 2 tablespoons maple flavoring
2 eggs, beaten
1 teaspoon salt
4 tablespoons oil
2 teaspoons baking powder

2 teaspoons angel cream or
  cream of tartar
2 cups milk or buttermilk
2 cups all-purpose or
  whole wheat flour
8 eggs
½ cup water
Salt to taste

In saucepan, heat together 1 cup water, butter, broth, stevia, and maple flavoring until butter fully melts. Pour into 9x13-inch pan. In bowl, blend 2 eggs, salt, oil, baking powder, angel cream, milk, and flour. Pour batter evenly over broth mixture, but do not stir. Bake at 350 degrees for about 30 minutes. In bowl, beat together 8 eggs, ½ cup water, and salt. Pour over hot cake and return to oven for 30 more minutes.

KAREN MILLER, *Monroe, WI*

Yogurt

2 tablespoons plain gelatin
½ cup water
1 gallon milk
1 cup sugar

½ cup plain yogurt
1 cup dry milk powder
Pie filling (optional)

Soak gelatin in water. Heat milk to 170 degrees then cool to 135 degrees. Add soaked gelatin, mixing until dissolved. Add sugar and plain yogurt; mix well. Put pan in "off" oven for 8 hours to incubate. Mix in dry milk powder. Flavor with your favorite pie filling.

LUELLA MILLER, *Shreve, OH*

Amish Sweets

Every culture has its own special foods, including sweets. The Amish are no exception. Attend any of their celebrations and you're bound to find all sorts of heavenly offerings, including shoofly pie, fried pies, whoopie pies, cakes, doughnuts, and a variety of cookies. All these items are mostly made from scratch with simple, wholesome ingredients.

Many Amish keep bees, so they can collect and sell the honey. Some of their desserts are sweetened with honey they have produced. Another favorite sweetener is molasses. Some of the best Amish pies and cookies include this thick, rich flavor. Still others use processed sugar and sweeteners, purchased in superstores or local groceries.

When it comes to flours and other grains, some of the Amish grind their own at home. Some choose manual mills with large flywheels. These require energy and discipline, traits most Amish women have in abundance.

Speaking of grains, most Amish bakers are known for their Friendship Bread. Typically, an Amish woman will share a cup of the liquid yeast culture (starter) with a friend. They keep this going from house to house, friend to friend, in much the same way a chain letter travels from place to place. This yummy cake-like bread is rich with cinnamon flavor. Many Amish cooks add to the base recipe with ingredients like bananas, coconut, nuts, or even chocolate.

Once the Amish housewife has the Friendship Bread recipe down pat, she can use it as a foundation for hundreds of other sweet treats like dump cakes, cookies, bars, muffins, and even biscotti. Of course, her first passion is to feed her family, but baking for local gatherings is pure delight and offers the women a way to share their creations and ideas—without being too boastful of course.

People in every culture love their sweets, and the Amish are no exception. What sets them apart is their use of local farm products, some as close as their own backyard beehive.

RECIPES FOR DESSERTS

My son, eat thou honey,
because it is good; and the
honeycomb, which is
sweet to thy taste.

PROVERBS 24:13

Cakes and Brownies

BUTTERNUT SQUASH BROWNIES

½ cup butternut squash puree
2 eggs
1 teaspoon vanilla
1 cup sugar
⅔ cup flour

½ cup cocoa
½ teaspoon baking powder
½ teaspoon salt
½ teaspoon cinnamon
1 cup chocolate chips

Combine puree, eggs, and vanilla in large mixing bowl. Stir in sugar and combine well. Add flour, cocoa, baking powder, salt, and cinnamon. Mix well. Stir in chocolate chips. Spoon batter into greased 8-inch square pan and bake at 350 degrees for 25 to 30 minutes.

BUTTERSCOTCH BROWNIES

2½ cups flour
1 teaspoon baking powder
½ teaspoon salt
2 sticks butter, softened
1¾ cups brown sugar

1 tablespoon vanilla
2 eggs
1 (11 ounce) package butterscotch-
    flavored chips
1 cup chopped pecans or walnuts

Combine flour, baking powder, and salt in medium bowl. Beat butter, sugar, and vanilla in large mixing bowl until creamy. Beat in eggs. Gradually add flour mixture to egg mixture. Stir in 1 cup of butterscotch chips, along with pecans. Spread into ungreased 9x13-inch baking pan. Sprinkle with remaining chips. Bake at 350 degrees for 30 to 40 minutes.

Debbie Cooper
Debbie enjoyed learning to make
these brownies for her family.

BREAD CUSTARD PUDDING

2 cups bread chunks
2½ cups milk
4 eggs
¾ cup sugar

¼ teaspoon salt
1 teaspoon vanilla
1 teaspoon nutmeg

Place bread in 1-quart baking dish. Scald milk. In separate bowl, beat eggs, sugar, salt, and vanilla. Mix well, then add milk to egg mixture. Pour over bread. Sprinkle with nutmeg. Place dish in larger pan with 1½ inches water. Bake at 350 degrees for 40 minutes.

BROWNIES

¾ cup flour
1 cup sugar
½ teaspoon baking powder
⅓ cup cocoa

½ cup margarine, melted
3 egg whites
1 teaspoon vanilla
½ cup chopped walnuts

Sift dry ingredients together in a bowl. Add margarine, egg whites, and vanilla; beat. Stir in nuts. Pour into lightly greased 8x8-inch pan. Bake at 350 degrees for 30 to 35 minutes. Cool and cut.

MRS. SAMUEL E. SCHWARTZ, *Geneva, IN*

Coconut Pecan Cake

Cake:

- 1 box white cake mix
- 1¼ cups water
- 4 eggs
- ½ cup oil
- 1 cup shredded coconut
- 1 cup diced pecans

Frosting/Topping:

- 4 tablespoons butter, divided
- 2 cups coconut
- 1 (8 ounce) package cream cheese, softened
- 2 teaspoons milk
- 3½ cups powdered sugar
- ½ teaspoon vanilla
- 1 cup chopped pecans

Blend cake mix with water, eggs, and oil until smooth. Stir in coconut and nuts. Pour into greased and floured 8-inch round pans and bake at 350 degrees for 35 minutes or until done. Cool completely. Melt 2 tablespoons butter in skillet. Add 2 cups coconut and stir constantly over low heat until golden brown. Allow coconut to cool. To make icing, cream 2 tablespoons butter with cream cheese. Add milk and powdered sugar alternately, beating well. Add vanilla, and stir in most of toasted coconut. Ice cake, and sprinkle with remaining coconut and nuts.

Lisa Brooks

Lisa has baked a lot of cakes in her career as a caterer, but this is one of her favorites. She's crazy about the combination of coconut and pecan, but the addition of cream cheese really tops it off.

GERMAN CHOCOLATE POUND CAKE

4 ounces Baker's German's Sweet
   Chocolate
2 cups sugar
1 cup shortening
4 eggs

1 cup buttermilk
2 teaspoons vanilla
3 cups flour
½ teaspoon baking soda
1 teaspoon salt

Melt chocolate in double boiler. Remove from heat and stir. Cool. In separate bowl, cream sugar and shortening. Add eggs and buttermilk. Add vanilla. Sift flour, baking soda, and salt. Add to shortening mixture and blend well. Stir in chocolate until incorporated. Pour into greased and floured 9-inch tube pan. Bake at 300 degrees for 1½ hours. Remove from pan to cool, then glaze as desired.

Lisa Brooks

Lisa's customers can't get enough of this rich chocolate cake!

HOT FUDGE PUDDING CAKE

1¼ cups sugar, divided
1 cup flour
6 tablespoons cocoa, divided
2 teaspoons baking powder
¼ teaspoon salt

½ cup milk
⅓ cup melted butter
1½ teaspoons vanilla
½ cup brown sugar
1¼ cups hot water

Stir together ¾ cup sugar, flour, 3 tablespoons cocoa, baking powder, and salt. Stir in milk, butter, and vanilla. Spread in greased square pan. Mix remaining ½ cup sugar, brown sugar, and 3 tablespoons cocoa. Sprinkle evenly over batter. Pour hot water over top. Do not stir. Bake at 350 degrees for 30 to 35 minutes.

Nichole Smith

*Nichole might be swamped with schoolwork, babysitting, and her
cooking classes, but she always makes time to cook this amazing
pudding cake for her siblings.*

Lazy Daisy Cake

Cake:

2 large eggs
1 cup sugar
1 cup flour
1 teaspoon baking powder
½ teaspoon salt
½ cup milk
1½ tablespoons butter

Topping:

¼ cup unsalted butter
½ cup plus 2 tablespoons brown sugar
¼ cup milk
1 cup coconut

In large mixing bowl, beat eggs until foamy. Add sugar, beating at high speed until mixture is thick. Stir in flour, baking powder, and salt. In saucepan, heat milk and butter together to boiling. Add to ingredients in bowl, beating to combine. Pour batter into greased and floured 8-inch round baking pan. Bake at 350 degrees for 30 minutes. Remove from oven and place on rack to cool. To make topping, melt butter in saucepan. Add brown sugar, milk, and coconut, then stir. Pour topping over warm cake. Place under broiler for 2 to 3 minutes or until topping is golden brown and bubbling.

Lisa Brooks

Another one of Lisa's favorites. She loves the addition of brown sugar in the topping.

Shortcake Delight

4 eggs, beaten
⅓ cup sugar
½ cup oil
2 tablespoons baking powder
2 teaspoons salt
2 cups milk, divided
4 cups flour

In bowl, stir together eggs, sugar, and oil. Add baking powder, salt, and 1 cup milk, mixing well. Add flour and remaining 1 cup milk. Mix well. Pour into greased 9x13-inch cake pan. Bake at 350 degrees for 15 to 18 minutes or until golden brown.

KAREN MILLER, *Monroe, WI*

"This recipe is easy enough for five-year-olds to make."

Our Favorite Angel Food Cake

2 cups egg whites
1½ teaspoons cream of tartar
1 pinch salt
1 cup sugar

2 teaspoons vanilla
1½ cups powdered sugar
1 cup cake flour

Beat egg whites; gradually sprinkle in cream of tartar and salt. When egg whites are stiff, add sugar and vanilla. In bowl, sift together powdered sugar and flour. Fold into egg mixture. Pour into ungreased angel food cake pan and bake at 350 degrees for 30 minutes until toothpick comes out clean. Do not over bake as that will cause a dry cake. Cool cake in upside-down pan.

Flavor options:

- Chocolate – exchange 1 cup flour for ½ cup cocoa and ½ cup flour

- Strawberry – exchange 1 cup sugar for ½ cup strawberry gelatin mix and ½ cup sugar

- Maple nut – exchange 2 teaspoons vanilla for ½ teaspoon maple flavoring and 1 teaspoon vanilla; add chopped walnuts

Verena N. Schwartz, *Scottsburg, IN*

STRAWBERRY SHORTCAKE

½ cup sugar
4 tablespoon butter, softened
1 egg, beaten
½ cup milk
½ teaspoon vanilla extract

1½ cups flour
2 teaspoons baking powder
Pinch of salt
Strawberries, sliced
Whipped cream

In a medium-size mixing bowl, cream sugar with butter. Then add egg, milk, and vanilla; mix well. Add the flour, baking powder, and salt; mix well. Pour into a greased 9-inch pie pan. Bake at 350 degrees for 25 to 30 minutes. Top with fresh strawberries and whipped cream.

Heidi Troyer

Supper Cake

1 cup cornmeal
½ cup oats
½ cup whole wheat or spelt flour
½ cup all-purpose flour
2 teaspoons baking powder
1 teaspoon salt
½ cup brown sugar
½ cup melted butter
1 teaspoon baking soda
1 cup sour milk
1 egg

Combine cornmeal, oats, flours, baking powder, salt, and sugar. Mix in butter. Dissolve baking soda in sour milk; add to first mixture. Add egg; mix well. Bake in 9x13-inch pan at 350 degrees for 30 minutes. Good served with fresh fruit and milk. We also like to dry the cake and crumble for a Grape-Nuts type of cereal.

TIP: To make sour milk, place 1 tablespoon vinegar in measuring cup. Fill with milk to 1 cup line. Let sit for about 5 minutes before adding to recipe.

SUSAN YODER, *Fultonville, NY*

White-as-Snow Cake

1½ cups flour
4½ teaspoons baking powder
1½ cups sugar
1 teaspoon salt
½ cup shortening, softened but not melted
1 cup milk, divided
4 egg whites
1 teaspoon vanilla

Sift dry ingredients into mixing bowl. Add shortening and ⅔ cup milk. Beat until batter is well blended and glossy. Add remaining milk, egg whites, and vanilla. Beat until smooth. Bake in two well-greased 8-inch round pans at 350 degrees for 30 minutes. Frost as desired.

ADA MAST, *Kalona, IA*

Candy

⸻ ⚬◦⚬ ⸻

CARAMELS

1 cup butter or margarine

1 pound light brown sugar

1 (14 ounce) can sweetened
  condensed milk

1 cup light corn syrup

1 pinch salt

1½ teaspoons vanilla

In heavy-bottomed saucepan over medium heat, combine butter, brown sugar, milk, corn syrup, and salt. Bring to a boil, stirring constantly. Heat to between 234 and 240 degrees, or until small amount of syrup dropped into cold water forms soft ball that flattens when removed from water and placed on flat surface. Cook for 2 minutes at that temperature. Remove from heat and stir in vanilla. Meanwhile, butter a 9x13-inch baking pan. When caramel is ready, pour into buttered pan. Allow to cool completely at room temperature. Remove from pan and cut into squares using scissors. Wrap individual pieces in waxed paper or plastic wrap.

Pecan Balls

2 cups flour	½ teaspoon vanilla
¼ cup sugar	2 cups finely chopped pecans
1 cup margarine	⅓ cup powdered sugar

Sift together into medium-sized bowl the flour and sugar. Work in margarine and vanilla with spoon or hands until well blended. Add pecans and mix well. Shape dough into 1-inch balls and place on ungreased pans. Bake at 325 degrees for about 25 minutes or until pale brown. When slightly cool, roll or shake in powdered sugar. Store in airtight container.

Nichole Smith

These have become a favorite of Nichole's siblings.

Cashew Brittle

2 cups sugar	3 cups cashews (roasted, salted, or unsalted)
1 cup light corn syrup	
½ cup water	1 teaspoon baking soda
1 cup butter	

In heavy saucepan, combine sugar, corn syrup, and water. Cook over medium-low heat until sugar dissolves, stirring occasionally. Add butter and stir until it melts. Cover. Cook over medium heat a couple of minutes to wash down sugar crystals from sides of pan. Uncover and cook to soft crack stage (280 degrees), stirring occasionally. Add cashews; cook, stirring constantly, until the mixture reaches hard crack stage (300 degrees). Remove from heat and stir in baking soda. Using great care not to burn yourself, quickly pour mixture evenly into two buttered 15x10x1-inch jelly roll pans and spread in thin layer. Let cool completely and then break into pieces. Store in airtight container.

Chocolate Caramels

1 cup butter
2¼ cups brown sugar
1 cup light corn syrup
1 (14 ounce) can sweetened
  condensed milk

1 teaspoon vanilla
1 pound milk chocolate
1 tablespoon butter

Melt 1 cup butter over medium heat in heavy 4-quart saucepan. Add brown sugar, corn syrup, and milk, stirring constantly until mixture reaches 242 to 248 degrees, or until small amount of syrup dropped into cold water forms soft ball. Remove from heat and stir in vanilla. Pour into buttered 8-inch square pan. When caramel has cooled and set, cut into 1-inch squares. Chill in refrigerator until firm. Melt chocolate with 1 tablespoon butter in double boiler or in bowl in microwave. Stir until smooth. Dip caramel squares in chocolate and place on waxed paper to cool.

Lisa Brooks

Lisa recently made a batch of these for a women's event, and they won rave reviews!

Toffee Candy

4 sticks butter
½ cup light corn syrup
2½ cups sugar

½ teaspoon salt
2 cups semi-sweet chocolate chips
1 cup chopped nuts

Melt butter in large pan. Add corn syrup. Gradually add sugar, then salt, stirring on high heat until mixture reaches hard crack stage (250 to 265 degrees). Pour onto two well-buttered baking sheets. While still hot, break chocolate bars into pieces and lay on top. When chocolate is soft, spread over candy, then quickly sprinkle on nuts. Cool and break into pieces.

Becky Blackburn

Becky makes this with her mom's help.

DIVINITY

½ cup corn syrup
2 cups sugar
½ cup water
¼ teaspoon salt

2 egg whites
Vanilla (optional)
Nuts (optional)

In saucepan with heavy bottom, combine corn syrup, sugar, water, and salt. Cook to hard ball stage (260 degrees). Beat egg whites. Slowly pour hot syrup into egg whites. Continue beating until it holds its shape. Add vanilla and nuts, if desired. Press into ungreased 9-inch square baking dish. Chill. Cut into small squares before completely firm.

Todd Collins

Todd never dreamed he'd fall in love with these dreamy white puffs of goodness, but he just couldn't help himself. They bring out the sweetness in him.

FUDGE MELTAWAYS

½ cup butter
1 ounce unsweetened chocolate
¼ cup sugar
1 teaspoon vanilla
1 egg
2 cups graham cracker crumbs
1 cup coconut

½ cup chopped walnuts
¼ cup butter
1 tablespoon milk
2 cups sifted powdered sugar
1 teaspoon vanilla
1½ ounces Baker's German's Sweet Chocolate

Melt ½ cup butter and unsweetened chocolate in saucepan. Add sugar, 1 teaspoon vanilla, egg, graham cracker crumbs, coconut, and nuts into mixture and incorporate well. Press into ungreased 9-inch square baking dish. Refrigerate. Mix ¼ cup butter, milk, powdered sugar, and 1 teaspoon vanilla. Spread over crumb mixture. Chill. Melt sweetened chocolate and spread evenly over chilled filling. Chill again. Cut into small squares before completely firm.

Trent Cooper

This is a recipe passed down from Trent's mother that he decided to try on his own.

CARAMEL CORN

2 cups brown sugar
½ cup light corn syrup
1 stick butter

¼ teaspoon cream of tartar
½ teaspoon baking soda
5 quarts salted popcorn

In saucepan, combine sugar, corn syrup, butter, and cream of tartar and cook at a low boil for 5 minutes. Remove from heat and add baking soda. Pour over popcorn. Mix well. Bake at 200 degrees for 1 hour.

Nichole Smith

It's easy to bring a smile to her siblings' faces when Nichole makes this special treat! She recommends adding a "surprise" like peanuts or M&M's.

Hard Candy

2 cups sugar
¾ cup light corn syrup
½ cup water

Flavoring
Coloring
1 cup powdered sugar

Bring sugar, corn syrup, and water to rolling boil. Keep boiling to hard crack stage (250 to 265 degrees). Add flavoring and coloring of your choice. Pour out onto baking sheet coated in powdered sugar. As syrup begins to cool, cut with scissors into pieces of desired size. Coat well in powdered sugar. Cool and place in airtight container.

Cocoa Fudge

2 cups powdered sugar
1¼ cups sugar
1½ cups milk
1 dash salt

1 tablespoon cocoa
1 teaspoon vanilla
1 cup pecans

Combine sugars, milk, salt, and cocoa in saucepan and cook until mixture holds a soft ball in cold water. Cool pan in larger pan of water. Add vanilla and nuts. Stir until mixture starts to thicken. Pour then press into buttered dish.

Peggy Ann Kimball

Peggy Ann can't help but fall in love when Heidi introduces her to this tasty fudge recipe.

Bars and Cookies

CINNAMON CREAM CHEESE SQUARES

2 (8 ounce) packages crescent rolls

1 cup sugar

2 (8 ounce) packages cream cheese, softened

¼ cup butter

¼ cup sugar mixed with 2 teaspoons cinnamon

Press out one package of crescent dough to cover the bottom of lightly greased 9x13-inch pan. Mix one cup of sugar and cream cheese together and spread over dough. Pat remaining dough over top. Melt butter and brush on top of dough then sprinkle with cinnamon sugar. Bake at 375 degrees for 25 minutes. Cool and cut into squares.

Kendra Perkins
This is a delicious and satisfying treat.

GERMAN CHOCOLATE BARS

1 (14 ounce) package individually wrapped caramels, unwrapped

⅓ cup sweetened condensed milk

1 box German chocolate cake mix

¾ cup butter, melted

½ cup sweetened condensed milk

1 cup semisweet chocolate chips

1 cup chopped walnuts

Preheat oven to 350 degrees. Grease and flour 9x13-inch pan. In saucepan, melt caramels with ⅓ cup milk. In separate bowl, combine cake mix with melted butter and ½ cup milk. Stir well. Spread half of cake batter in pan and bake for 6 to 8 minutes. Remove from oven and cover with caramel milk, chips, and nuts. Put remaining cake batter on top. Bake for another 10 minutes.

Coconut Love Bars

1 cup flour
3 tablespoons brown sugar
1 stick butter
1½ cups coconut

2 cups flour
⅔ cup raisins
⅔ cup chopped pecans or walnuts

Mix flour, sugar, butter, and coconut and pat evenly in greased 9x15-inch pan. Bake at 325 degrees for 10 minutes. Mix remaining ingredients and pour over baked crumbs. Bake 30 minutes. Cool and cut into squares.

Darren Keller and Ellen Blackburn
Darren and Ellen enjoy these coconut love bars that remind them of their newfound relationship.

Healthy Granola Bars

2½ cups old-fashioned oats
1½ cups quick oats
1½ cups Rice Krispies
1 cup flaxseed
Raisins (optional)

Chocolate chips (optional)
1½ cups peanut butter
1¼ cups honey
4 tablespoons melted butter

Mix all dry ingredients together. Blend peanut butter, honey, and butter for sauce. Pour over dry ingredients and mix well. Pour into pan and flatten.

MARY ANN SHROCK, *Danville, OH*

Chewy Chocolate Bars

1 cup almond butter or peanut butter
3 cups coconut
⅔ cup cocoa
⅔ cup raw honey

1 teaspoon salt
½ teaspoon vanilla
½ cup almond flour (optional)

Place all ingredients in food processor and blend until combined. Spread in shallow dish and refrigerate until firm. Option: Top with chocolate chips or chopped nuts.

Christina Peight, *Belleville, PA*

Pecan Bars

2 tablespoons butter
1 cup brown sugar
5 tablespoons flour
1 dash baking soda

1 cup chopped pecans
2 eggs
1 teaspoon vanilla
Powdered sugar

Melt butter in 8-inch square pan in 350-degree oven. Mix brown sugar, flour, baking soda, and pecans. In medium bowl, beat eggs until frothy and add vanilla. Stir brown sugar mixture into eggs; pour batter over butter. Do not stir. Bake at 350 degrees for 20 to 25 minutes. Let cool. Sprinkle with powdered sugar. Cut into bars.

Chocolate Chip Cookies

3 cups butter

4 cups sugar

6 eggs

2 teaspoons baking soda

1 teaspoon salt

2 teaspoons maple flavoring

1 cup chocolate chips

8½ cups flour

In a large bowl, cream butter and sugar. Add eggs, baking soda, salt, and maple flavoring; add chocolate chips. Then add enough flour to be able to form nice balls. Flatten balls with a glass dipped in sugar. Bake at 375 degrees for 10 to 12 minutes.

CEVILLA SWARTZENTRUBER, *Navarre, OH*

Jumbo Raisin Cookies

2 cups raisins

1 cup water

2 cups sugar

1 cup butter

2 eggs

1½ teaspoons vanilla

3½ cups flour

1½ teaspoons baking powder

1 teaspoon baking soda

1½ teaspoons salt

1 teaspoon cinnamon

In saucepan, boil raisins in water for 5 minutes. Cool. In mixing bowl, beat together sugar and butter. Add eggs and vanilla; mix well. Stir in dry ingredients. Mix in raisins with liquid. Drop by teaspoon onto baking sheet. Bake at 325 degrees for 16 to 17 minutes. Very soft and delicious!

RHONDA RAPP, *Crofton, KY*

Simple Peanut Butter Oatmeal Cookies

⅔ cup peanut butter (may substitute almond or cashew butter)

½ cup molasses or honey

2 teaspoons vanilla

2 cups oats

Mix peanut butter and molasses until smooth. Add vanilla and oats. Form into balls and place on greased baking sheet. Flatten. Bake at 350 degrees for 8 to 9 minutes.

PHEBE PEIGHT, *McVeytown, PA*

Peanut Butter Fingers

1⅛ cup butter
1⅛ cup sugar
1¼ cup brown sugar
¾ cup peanut butter
2 eggs

1½ teaspoons vanilla
½ teaspoon baking soda
2¼ cups flour
2¼ cups oatmeal

In a large mixing bowl, cream butter, sugars, and peanut butter. Add eggs and vanilla, mixing well. Mix in baking soda, flour, and oatmeal. Pat dough into greased 9x13-inch pan and bake at 350 degrees for 18 to 20 minutes.

Frosting:

⅜ cup milk
¼ cup peanut butter
2 cups powdered sugar

1½ teaspoons vanilla
¼ cup cocoa

Heat milk and peanut butter in a saucepan over low heat until dissolved. Add sugar, vanilla, and cocoa. Spread on cooled bars. Cut into long, thin bars.

Lisa Brooks

Lisa found these bars to be a hit with children.

Double Treat Cookies

1 cup peanut butter
1 cup shortening
2 cups white or brown sugar
2 eggs
2 cups flour

2 teaspoons baking soda
½ teaspoon salt
1 cup chopped nuts
1 cup chocolate chips

Cream peanut butter, shortening, and sugar. Mix in eggs. Add flour, baking soda, and salt. Fold in nuts and chocolate chips. Shape dough into small balls. Place on baking sheet. Flatten with glass dipped in sugar. Bake at 350 degrees for 10 to 12 minutes. Yield: approximately 50 cookies.

SARAH D. F. SCHWARTZ, *Galesburg, KS*

Date Pinwheels

½ cup butter
½ cup brown sugar
½ cup sugar
1 egg
½ teaspoon vanilla
2 cups flour
½ teaspoon baking soda

½ teaspoon salt
1 cup chopped walnuts or pecans
Filling:
1 pound pitted dates, chopped
½ cup sugar
½ cup water

Cream butter, sugars, egg, and vanilla. Add dry ingredients. Chill dough. While dough is chilling, combine dates, ½ cup sugar, and water in saucepan and cook until thick (2 to 3 minutes). Remove dough from refrigerator and roll to ¼-inch thick, then spread date mixture on top. Roll up and chill. Slice and bake at 375 degrees for 10 to 12 minutes.

Ellen Blackburn
A great project she and Darren did
on a family date with the kids.

SNICKERDOODLES

1 cup shortening
1½ cups sugar
2 eggs
2¾ cups flour
2 teaspoons cream of tartar

1 teaspoon baking soda
¼ teaspoon salt
2 tablespoons sugar
2 tablespoons cinnamon

Mix shortening, 1½ cups sugar, and eggs. Blend flour, cream of tartar, baking soda, and salt. Stir all together. Shape dough into 1-inch balls. Combine 2 tablespoons sugar with 2 tablespoons cinnamon and roll dough in mixture. Place 2 inches apart on ungreased baking sheet, lined with parchment paper. Bake at 400 degrees for 8 to 10 minutes.

Charlene Higgins

Finally! A recipe simple enough, even a cook like Charlene can manage. These crisp cookies are as light as air—and guaranteed to win over even the toughest mother-in-law.

Pumpkin Whoopie Pies

2 cups brown sugar	1 teaspoon salt
1 cup oil	1 teaspoon baking powder
1½ cups pumpkin (cooked or canned)	1 teaspoon baking soda
2 eggs	1½ tablespoons cinnamon
1 teaspoon vanilla	½ tablespoon ginger
3 cups flour	½ tablespoon cloves

Cream sugar and oil together in mixing bowl. Add pumpkin, eggs, and vanilla. Mix well. Add dry ingredients and stir until combined. Drop by heaping teaspoon onto greased baking sheet. Bake at 350 degrees for 10 to 12 minutes.

Filling:

2 egg whites	¼ teaspoon salt
1½ cups shortening	4½ cups powdered sugar
1 teaspoon vanilla	

In bowl, beat egg whites and add shortening, vanilla, and salt until combined well. Stir in the powdered sugar and mix until creamy. Spread a couple tablespoons of filling on each cookie. Place another cookie on top of filling. Wrap each "sandwich" in plastic wrap.

Heidi Troyer

Who can say no to pumpkin, especially during autumn?

Cream Puffs

1 cup water	½ teaspoon salt
½ cup butter	4 eggs
1 cup flour	

In saucepan, boil water and butter until butter melts. Add flour and salt all at once. Stir until dough forms a ball. Remove from heat. Add 1 egg, beat, and let stand 5 minutes. Add remaining eggs one at a time, beating after each. Let stand 10 minutes. Drop by teaspoon onto baking sheet and bake at 375 degrees for 20 to 25 minutes.

Pies

PIECRUST

2 cups flour

1 dash salt

3 tablespoons sugar

1 cup chilled butter or shortening

½ cup water

Stir flour, salt, and sugar together in large bowl. Cut butter or shortening into dry mixture using pastry cutter or by pinching fat into mixture with your hands. Add water. Form into ball. Chill and roll, then place in pie pan.

Heidi Troyer

Heidi's "no-fail" piecrust is a recipe she's happy to share.

FUNERAL PIE

2 cups raisins

2 cups water, divided

½ cup light brown sugar

½ cup sugar

3 tablespoons cornstarch

1½ teaspoons cinnamon

¼ teaspoon allspice

1 pinch salt

1 tablespoon cider vinegar

3 tablespoons butter

2 sheets pie dough

Combine raisins and ⅔ cup water in medium saucepan and heat over medium heat for 5 minutes. Combine sugars, cornstarch, spices, and salt in medium bowl and, stirring constantly, gradually add remaining 1⅓ cups water. Add this mixture to raisins. Cook and stir until mixture starts to bubble. Add vinegar and butter and heat until butter is melted. Cool. Line 9-inch pie pan with 1 sheet of dough leaving ½-inch overhang. Pour filling into crust. Place second sheet of dough on top of pie and trim to a 1-inch overhang. Fold dough under and crimp edge. Cut decorative slash marks into top crust to vent. Bake at 400 degrees until golden brown, about 15 minutes. Remove from oven and let cool completely.

Coconut Chess Pie

1¼ cups sugar	2 eggs
1 tablespoon cornstarch	1 tablespoon flour
½ stick butter, melted	¾ cup milk
1 cup coconut	1 teaspoon vanilla
1 dash salt	1 (9 inch) unbaked pastry shell

Stir all ingredients together and pour into pastry shell. Bake at 350 degrees for 45 minutes or until set.

Peach Cobbler

½ cup butter	3 teaspoons baking powder
1 cup flour	1 cup milk
2 cups sugar, divided	3 cups sliced fresh peaches
½ teaspoon salt	1 teaspoon cinnamon

Melt butter in baking dish. Sift flour, 1 cup sugar, salt, and baking powder together. Blend in milk. Pour over melted butter. Spread peaches over this and sprinkle with 1 cup sugar mixed with cinnamon. Bake at 350 degrees for 1 hour.

Miranda Cooper

Miranda loves peach pie, but this is easier to make.

Peanut Butter Pie

¾ cup sugar
1 cup peanut butter
1 (8 ounce) package cream cheese, softened

8 ounces whipped topping
2 teaspoons butter, melted
2 teaspoons vanilla
1 (9 inch) baked pastry shell

Cream together sugar, peanut butter, and cream cheese. Mix in whipped topping, butter, and vanilla. Pour into piecrust. Chill. Can be frozen.

BARBARA WENGERD, *Willshire, OH*

Chocolate Pie

1 cup sugar
2 tablespoons cocoa
¼ cup cornstarch
1 dash salt
2½ cups milk

3 tablespoons butter
3 egg yolks, beaten
1 teaspoon vanilla
1 (9 inch) baked pastry shell
Whipped cream

In medium saucepan, combine sugar, cocoa, cornstarch, salt, milk, and butter. Cook on stovetop (or microwave) until pudding consistency. Add egg yolks and vanilla, cook 1 additional minute, then whisk until smooth. Pour into piecrust and top with whipped cream.

Lance Freemont
Kids—and men—of all ages love a good chocolate pie, and this one takes the cake (pun intended).

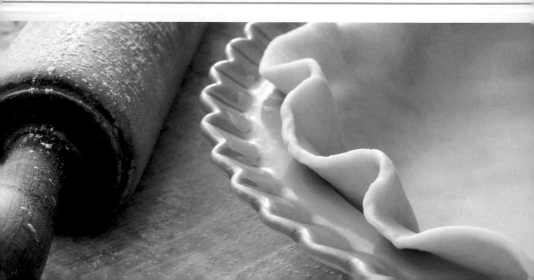

PINEAPPLE PIE

1 (20 ounce) can crushed pineapple
    with juice
2 teaspoons cornstarch
1 (8 ounce) package cream cheese,
    softened
⅓ cup sugar

1 cup sour cream
1 teaspoon vanilla
Medium tub whipped topping
Piecrust of your choice (traditional or
    graham cracker crust)

Pour pineapple into bowl. Thicken with cornstarch. Place bowl in refrigerator to chill. In separate bowl, mix cream cheese, sugar, sour cream, and vanilla. Fold in whipped topping. Fill baked piecrust and top with cooled, thickened pineapple.

Lisa Brooks

Lisa recommends this recipe for outdoor summer gatherings.

APPLE CREAM PIE

3 cups finely chopped apples
1 cup brown sugar
¼ teaspoon salt

1 rounded tablespoon flour
1 cup cream
1 (9 inch) unbaked pastry shell

Mix apples, brown sugar, salt, flour, and cream. Put in unbaked pastry shell. Bake at 450 degrees for 15 minutes. Reduce heat to 325 degrees for an additional 30 to 40 minutes. When pie is about half done, take knife and push top apples down to soften. After pie cools, store in refrigerator.

Heidi Troyer

This pie is particularly good to take on outings.
Heidi recommends you share it with those you love.

SHOOFLY PIE

2 cups flour
1½ cups brown sugar
2 rounded tablespoons butter
2 cups molasses

2 eggs
2 cups hot water, divided
2 teaspoons baking soda
2 (9 inch) unbaked pastry shells

Mix flour, sugar, and butter; set aside 1 cup for crumbs. To first mixture, add molasses, eggs, and 1½ cups hot water. Mix baking soda into ½ cup hot water; add to first mixture, blending well. Divide batter evenly between pastry shells. Bake at 375 degrees for 45 minutes. Serve warm with whipped cream or ice cream.

VERA MAST, *Kalona, IA*

YOGURT PIE

1 (14 ounce) can sweetened condensed milk
1 (8 ounce) package cream cheese, softened
1 quart strawberry or raspberry yogurt

1 large tub whipped topping
3 tablespoons lemon juice
Red food coloring (optional)
3 graham cracker piecrusts

Mix milk, cream cheese, yogurt, whipped topping, and lemon juice together well. Add a few drops red food coloring if desired. Pour into piecrusts. Refrigerate until ready to serve.

ANNA GINGERICH, *Kimbolton, OH*

IMPOSSIBLE-TO-RUIN PIE

2 cups milk
4 eggs, beaten
½ teaspoon salt
1 tablespoon vanilla

½ cup flour
½ cup sweetener (sugar, honey, or maple syrup)
1 cup coconut

Blend everything together. Pour into glass pie pan. Bake at 350 degrees for 45 minutes just until set. No piecrust needed!

RACHEL YODER, *Fultonville, NY*

Raisin Nut Pie

1½ cups sugar

3 tablespoons vinegar

½ teaspoon cinnamon

¼ cup chopped pecans or walnuts

3 tablespoons melted butter

3 tablespoons water

4 eggs, beaten

1 cup raisins (or dried cranberries)

1 (9 inch) unbaked pastry shell

Combine all ingredients. Pour into pastry shell, and bake at 425 degrees for 10 minutes. Reduce heat to 350 degrees and bake for 20 to 30 minutes.

Fried Pies

2 teaspoons shortening

1 cup sifted flour

1 egg yolk

3 tablespoons hot milk

⅛ teaspoon salt

1 to 1½ cups fruit filling

In mixing bowl, cut shortening into flour. Add egg, milk, and salt and mix well. Knead well to make smooth dough. Roll dough to ⅛-inch thick. Cut into rounds. Cover half of each circle with fruit filling of choice, leaving a ¼-inch edge. Fold circles over and pinch edges. Fry in deep fat. Best while hot. Or make glaze when cooled to maintain moister filling. Makes 6 to 8 pies.

Heidi Troyer

A top seller at bake sales.

Puddings

BREAD PUDDING

2 eggs, beaten
½ cup sugar
2 cups milk

1 teaspoon vanilla
2 tablespoons butter
2 cups bread cubes

In mixing bowl, combine all ingredients. Spread into greased 8-inch square pan. Bake at 350 degrees for 35 to 45 minutes or until top springs back when touched.

SAUCE:

2 cups water
1 cup sugar
1 tablespoon butter

1 large lemon, juiced
1 tablespoon cornstarch
1 egg yolk

Combine ingredients in saucepan and cook until desired consistency. Pour over bread pudding and serve.

Kendra Perkins
Talk about the perfect comfort food!
This is one of Kendra's favorites.

Banana Pudding

1 small box vanilla instant pudding

2 cups milk

1 box vanilla wafer cookies

2 to 3 ripe bananas, sliced

1 tub whipped topping, thawed (or whipping cream and sugar, to make your own)

Prepare pudding according to package instructions, blending mix with milk. Chill. Place vanilla wafers in single layer on bottom of small baking dish. Spread half of prepared pudding over cookies. Top pudding with single layer of banana slices. Repeat layers, starting with cookies. Top final layer of banana slices with whipped topping. Refrigerate at least 1 hour before serving.

Randy and Marsha Olsen
Heidi's foster children enjoy this recipe because they can help her make it.

Old-Fashioned Graham Pudding

1 quart milk

¾ cup brown sugar

⅔ cup flour

1 pinch salt

1 egg

Milk

1 sleeve graham crackers

3 tablespoons brown sugar

¼ cup butter, melted

1 tub whipped topping

In saucepan, heat 1 quart milk. In bowl, combine ¾ cup brown sugar, flour, salt, and egg with a little milk to moisten. Stir into heated milk. Bring to a rolling boil to thicken. Let cool. Crush graham crackers; add 3 tablespoons brown sugar and butter. Layer pudding into serving dish. Start with half of pudding then half of graham crackers then half of whipped topping; repeat.

MATTIE YODER, *Millersburg, OH*

BUTTERSCOTCH TAPIOCA

¼ cup butter
½ cup chopped nuts
2 cups brown sugar
4 cups water

¾ cup baby pearl tapioca
½ teaspoon salt
3 teaspoons maple flavoring
1 tub whipped topping

In saucepan, melt butter until brown. Add nuts and sugar; stir until moist. Add water and bring to a boil. Add tapioca and cook 15 to 20 minutes. Add salt and flavoring. Cool. Mix in whipped topping.

FANNIE MILLER, *Middlefield, OH*

CHERRY PUDDING

1 (14.5 ounce) can pitted tart
    cherries, undrained
1 cup sugar
1 cup flour

1 egg
1 teaspoon baking soda
½ cup nuts

Mix all ingredients well, then put into greased 11x7-inch glass dish. Bake at 350 degrees for 30 to 35 minutes.

Marsha Olsen
An easy dump recipe someone as young as Marsha can help with.

CHOCOLATE CHIA SEED PUDDING

3 tablespoons chia seeds
1 cup milk (dairy or nut)

1½ to 3 teaspoons cocoa
1 tablespoon maple syrup

Stir all ingredients in small bowl. Cover and refrigerate for 4 hours or overnight.

CHRISTINA PEIGHT, *Belleville, PA*
"This is so basic and simple! My children love the chocolate pudding. If you don't like the tapioca texture, just run the ingredients through a blender."

Icings, Creams, and Sweet Sauces

Beat-and-Eat Icing

3 egg whites
¾ cup sugar
¼ teaspoon cream of tartar

1 teaspoon vanilla
¼ cup boiling water

In mixing bowl, beat all ingredients together until thick. Use as you would whipped topping.

ENOS AND LYDIA YODER, *Fredericksburg, OH*

Caramel Icing

1 (16 ounce) box light brown sugar
1 cup half-and-half

4 tablespoons butter
1 teaspoon vanilla

In saucepan, combine sugar, half-and-half, and butter. Boil until soft ball forms. Add vanilla. Beat until thickened. Spread at once.

CREAM CHEESE MAPLE FROSTING

1 (8 ounce) package cream cheese
2 tablespoons butter

¼ cup cocoa (optional)
½ cup maple syrup (approximate)

Whip together cream cheese, butter, and cocoa. Drizzle in maple syrup until desired consistency. If it gets too runny, put in refrigerator for a few minutes.

CHRISTINA PEIGHT, *Belleville, PA*

FUDGE SAUCE

½ cup butter
4 ounces Baker's German's Sweet
  Chocolate
1 cup sugar

1 (5 ounce) can evaporated milk
1 tablespoon light corn syrup
⅛ teaspoon salt
1 teaspoon vanilla

In saucepan, melt butter and chocolate over low heat. Stir in sugar, milk, corn syrup, and salt. Cook over medium heat, stirring gently for 5 minutes or until sugar dissolves and sauce is smooth. Stir in vanilla. Cool. Cover and chill up to one month. Serve on ice cream and other treats.

Denise McGuire
A chocolate drizzle makes everything better!

Amish Canning

Nothing takes you back in time like the home-canning process. Visit any Amish household and you will find the cupboards stocked full of vegetables, fruits, jams, jellies, butters, relishes, chow-chow, pickles, and the like, most canned by the women of the house, a good friend, or a relative.

Canning is, in many ways, an art form, one passed down from generation to generation. This is especially true in Amish communities, where girls are taught by their mothers, grandmothers, aunts, and other women how to preserve the foods grown on their land.

Some Amish can hundreds of quarts of food every single year. Those with large gardens have a particularly large stash of goodies, but even women who don't have gardens have ready access to an abundance of fruits and vegetables at their local produce stands.

Consider the practicality of canning for the Amish family: To make a "quick trip" to the grocery store often requires prepping horse and buggy, then making your way to town. Picture this in the dead of winter, in the bitter cold. To have a stocked pantry is to keep your family healthy.

On canning day, the Amish women start with cleanliness and sanitation. No detail is overlooked as the jars and lids are boiled and cleaned. Even the tiniest nick in a jar could prove deadly, so bad jars are tossed. Canners work with a "safety first" motto in mind.

Typically, Amish cold pack their food, placing it directly into the jars without cooking first. (Note: This is not a practice the USDA considers safe but is the method the Amish have been using for generations.) Boiling water is added, and the cans are firmly sealed. The jars are submerged in a water bath, which is brought to a boil. The USDA recommends the use of a pressure cooker, which some Amish women do have and use for certain foods.

The canning process might be considered tedious by some, but when working alongside friends and neighbors, the time passes quickly. And there's nothing finer than eating jams, jellies, fruits, or vegetables that you have canned yourself.

RECIPES FOR SPREADS AND PICKLES

———— ⟜∘⟐∘⟜ ————

*And God said, Let the earth
bring forth grass, the herb yielding
seed, and the fruit tree yielding fruit
after his kind, whose seed is in itself,
upon the earth: and it was so.*

GENESIS 1:11

———— ⟜∘⟐∘⟜ ————

Apple Butter

8 apples, peeled
1 cup apple cider
1½ cups sugar, divided

¾ teaspoon cinnamon
¼ teaspoon cloves

Cut apples into 1-inch pieces. In Dutch oven or heavy saucepan, bring apples, cider, and ½ cup sugar to a rolling boil over high heat. Cover, leaving lid slightly ajar. Boil for 20 minutes or until apples are tender, stirring every 5 minutes. Most of liquid will evaporate. Process cooked apples and cooking liquid in blender until smooth. Return mixture to Dutch oven. Add cinnamon, cloves, and remaining 1 cup sugar. Stir. Bring to a boil over high heat. Reduce heat to low and simmer uncovered, while stirring often, for 15 minutes or until thickened. Cool and store in airtight containers in refrigerator.

Honey Butter

1 stick butter, softened   *½ cup honey*

Whip butter with mixer until light and fluffy, then add honey and beat until well incorporated. Wonder served on biscuits.

Kevin Cooper
Here's an easy recipe Kevin can help with
and he loves to eat it on biscuits.

Peach Butter

14 cups peeled and coarsely chopped   *4½ teaspoons lemon juice*
fresh or frozen peaches (about 5½   *1½ teaspoons cinnamon*
pounds)   *¾ teaspoon cloves*
2½ cups sugar   *½ cup quick-cooking tapioca*

In large bowl, combine peaches, sugar, lemon juice, cinnamon, and cloves. Transfer to slow cooker. Cover and cook on low for 8 to 10 hours or until peaches are very soft, stirring occasionally. Stir in tapioca. Cook uncovered on high for 1 hour or until thickened. Pour into jars or freezer containers; cool to room temperature, about 1 hour. Cover and refrigerate up to three weeks.

Carrot Marmalade

1 large orange, finely shredded   *2 cups grated carrots*
1 large lemon, finely shredded   *2½ cups sugar*
2 cups water

Combine lemon and orange shreds in large pot with water. Boil over medium high heat for 10 minutes. Add carrots and sugar. Continue boiling until marmalade is thick and forms a sheet when poured from the spoon (approximately 30 minutes). Seal the marmalade in sterilized jars and process in boiling water for 5 minutes.

Apple Cinnamon Jelly

1 quart apple juice
1 box Sure-Jell

4½ cups sugar
2 tablespoons Red Hots
    cinnamon candies

In saucepan, combine juice and Sure-Jell and bring to a rolling boil. Add sugar and cinnamon candies, cooking until candies dissolve. Stir and continue to cook for another couple of minutes, then pour into canning jars and seal.

Loretta Donnelly
Loretta borrowed this recipe from Heidi but added
a fun new twist—cinnamon candies!

Apricot Jam (No Pectin)

2½ pounds ripe apricots (10 cups
    prepared)
½ cup sugar

Juice of 1 lemon
1 splash water

Wash, halve, and pit apricots. Place all ingredients in saucepan over high heat without lid. When mixture begins to bubble, turn burner down to lowest heat setting. Cook 3 to 4 hours, stirring occasionally. Pour into canning jars and seal.

Harvest Jam

1½ cups peeled and chopped plums
    (about 6)
1½ cups peeled and chopped pears
    (about 3)
3 cups peeled and chopped apples

(about 2)
1 cup peeled and chopped oranges
    (about 2)
1 cup apple cider
3½ cups sugar

Combine all ingredients. Cover and refrigerate overnight. The following day, cook until mixture gels. Seal in jars while hot. Either process in canner or store in refrigerator.

Pickles and Relish

Beet Pickles

1 quart small beets
2 cups sugar

1 pint vinegar

Cook beets, then skin and slice. Put beets into pan with sugar and vinegar and bring to a boil. Simmer for a few minutes, then place in canning jars. Seal with a water bath.

Bread and Butter Pickles

4 quarts sliced cucumbers
6 medium onions, sliced
3 cloves garlic, minced
2 sweet peppers, chopped
⅓ cup canning salt
Ice

5 cups sugar
1½ cups turmeric
1½ teaspoons celery seed
2 teaspoons mustard seed
3 cups cider vinegar

Combine cucumbers, onions, garlic, peppers, and salt and cover with ice for 3 hours. Drain thoroughly and add remaining ingredients. Heat to a boil. Makes 8 pints to can.

Icebox Pickles

2 cups white sugar
1 cup white vinegar
1 tablespoon salt
½ teaspoon turmeric
½ teaspoon celery seed

1 teaspoon dry mustard
6 cups sliced cucumbers
1 cup onion, sliced
Dill seed

Bring sugar, vinegar, salt, turmeric, celery seed, and dry mustard to a boil on stove. Pack cucumbers and sliced onions into canning jars and pour boiling syrup over them, then add dill seed. Seal in water bath canner.

Pickled Okra

2 cups cider vinegar	1 teaspoon coriander seed
1 cup water	1 teaspoon celery seed
1 tablespoon sugar	1 teaspoon whole peppercorns
2 tablespoons kosher salt	3 pints okra
6 cloves garlic, minced	3 small hot peppers

Combine vinegar, water, sugar, salt, garlic, coriander, celery seed, and peppercorns in nonreactive pot and bring to a boil. Reduce heat to keep brine warm. Place three pint jars and accompanying lids in water bath and bring to a boil for 10 minutes. Remove jars from bath. Pack full with okra. Return water to a boil. Place 1 hot pepper in each jar. Pour brine into jars to cover okra. Cap tightly and return jars to bath of boiling water for 15 minutes to seal.

CORN RELISH

Kernels from 10 ears fresh yellow
    sweet corn

2 large red sweet peppers, finely
    chopped

2 large green sweet peppers, finely
    chopped

8 stalks celery, diced

1 large yellow onion, diced

4 cups cider vinegar

2 cups sugar

¾ teaspoon dry mustard

3 teaspoons salt

4 whole allspice berries

Combine all ingredients in saucepan and bring to a boil. Stir until sugar dissolves. Reduce heat and simmer, uncovered, for about 20 minutes until vegetables are tender. Transfer relish to hot sterilized jars and seal with lids. Process jars in water bath for 10 minutes. Keep stored in dark, cool place.

PICKLE RELISH

2 cups finely chopped cucumber
½ cup finely chopped onion
¾ teaspoon salt
½ cup vinegar

¼ cup sugar
¼ teaspoon salt
1 teaspoon cornstarch
  dissolved in 1 teaspoon water

Toss cucumber and onion with ¾ teaspoon salt in colander over bowl and drain 3 hours. Discard liquid from bowl. Wrap cucumber and onion in a paper towel and squeeze out as much liquid as possible. Bring vinegar, sugar, and ¼ teaspoon salt to a boil in small heavy saucepan. Stir until sugar has dissolved. Boil until reduced to about ½ cup (3 to 4 minutes). Add cucumber-onion mixture and simmer, stirring constantly, for 2 minutes. Stir cornstarch mixture, then incorporate into relish. Continue stirring while simmering for 1 minute. Transfer relish to bowl and chill uncovered until cold, about 1½ hours.

CHOW-CHOW RELISH

2 cups frozen carrots
2 cups frozen cauliflower
2 cups frozen cut green beans
2 cups frozen cut yellow wax beans
1 (15 ounce) can kidney beans
1 large onion, diced
½ red sweet pepper, diced

½ teaspoon celery seed
¼ teaspoon turmeric
½ teaspoon salt
2½ cups sugar
1 cup vinegar
2 cups water

Combine all ingredients until fully incorporated. Chill and serve.

Lyle Troyer

*Lyle will be the first to tell you that pride is a sin,
but he's secretly proud of his wife, Heidi,
for making the best chow-chow in the district.*

Green Tomato Relish

1 quart chopped green tomato
1 large sweet onion, chopped
1 large green sweet pepper, chopped
2 tablespoons canning salt
1 cup sugar

1 tablespoon prepared mustard
1 teaspoon celery salt
4 whole cloves
1 cup vinegar

Combine tomatoes, onion, and pepper in large bowl. Sprinkle salt over vegetables. Let stand 1 hour. Drain vegetables. Combine drained vegetables, sugar, mustard, and celery salt in large pot. Tie cloves in cheesecloth and add to mixture. Stir in vinegar. Simmer for 20 minutes. Remove spice bag. Pack hot relish into hot jars and process for 10 minutes in hot water bath.

Pear Relish

1 gallon unpeeled and ground pears
½ gallon ground white onion
4 green sweet peppers, seeded and
    ground
2 red sweet peppers, seeded and
    ground

4 hot peppers, seeded and ground
2 tablespoons mustard seed
2 tablespoons turmeric
4 cups sugar
1 quart vinegar
1 cup salt

In large pot, combine pears with onion, peppers, and other ingredients. Cook low and slow until tender. Pour into canning jars and process for 15 minutes in hot water bath.

Loretta Donnelly

Loretta would like to send a personal thank-you to Heidi Troyer for passing along this recipe, which has become one of her favorite canning projects.

Amish Gatherings and Events

As a rule, most people are social beings. These days, most of us connect with those around us through social media. We text, private message, or post online in order to communicate. Spending time with those we love is complicated due to our busy lives and miles of physical separation.

The Amish see things differently. They would balk at the concept of communicating only from a distance, choosing instead to actually be together, to show up for one another, in good times and in bad. As a result, Amish women are rarely lonely. They are surrounded by a network of other women in their district. "Visiting" is just that. . .visiting. They sit and chat over a cup of tea or coffee. They work together on a quilt. They can jams and jellies. They exchange recipes. They pass along their skills. In short, they share life together.

The Amish give the word community new meaning. They live in community. They learn in community. They thrive in community.

They also celebrate in community. Whether it's visiting the mother of a new baby or attending a barn raising, a sewing bee, a Sunday night singing, or a wedding, the Amish know how to create food-filled gatherings. There's a casserole for every occasion, from a special When-the-Bishop-Calls Casserole to a Funeral Pie when someone passes away.

Among the favorite foods at big get-togethers are barbecue chicken (a staple), roasted corn, pickles and other canned goods (including pickled beets), potatoes, Amish Haystack, and baked goods. Lots and lots of baked goods. At a particularly large gathering, you might find the food table decked out with dozens of breads, rolls, pies, doughnuts, and cakes.

More than anything, the Amish enjoy good old-fashioned fellowship. They are relational, from childhood through their golden years.

RECIPES FOR MAIN DISHES

Heap on wood, kindle the fire,
consume the flesh, and spice it well,
and let the bones be burned.

EZEKIEL 24:10

Amish Haystack

½ pound saltine crackers or 1 bag corn chips, crushed

2 cups cooked rice (white or brown)

2 heads lettuce, chopped

1 (6 ounce) can black olives, sliced

2 cups diced tomatoes

2 cups diced onion

2 cups diced green sweet pepper

2 cups diced celery (optional)

1 quart cooked navy or pinto beans

2 eggs, boiled and chopped up (optional)

2 cups chopped nuts (optional)

2 cans cream of cheddar soup

1 (14 ounce) can condensed milk

3 pounds ground beef, browned

1 (16 ounce) jar spaghetti sauce or salsa

Put each of first eleven ingredients into separate containers. Mix soup and milk together in saucepan and heat. Combine ground beef and spaghetti sauce or salsa and heat. Each person creates their own haystack by layering items in order given on their plate. Pour cheese sauce and favorite salad dressing on top and enjoy! Serves 12 to 14 people.

Heidi Troyer

Heidi recommends this dish for a large crowd. Perfect for barn raisings and such.

Amish Beef Stroganoff

2 tablespoons butter

1 pound ground beef

1 tablespoon garlic salt

½ cup diced onion

1 tablespoon flour

1 can cream of chicken soup

1 (4 ounce) can mushrooms, undrained

1 teaspoon salt

¼ teaspoon pepper

1 cup sour cream

Noodles, cooked

In large skillet, melt butter. Add ground beef, garlic salt, and onion and cook until meat is done. Stir in flour. Add soup, mushrooms, salt, and pepper. Heat through, then add sour cream. Serve over noodles.

Miranda Cooper

Here's an easy meal to put a smile on each family's member's face.

BAKED STUFFED TOMATOES

6 slices bacon
6 medium tomatoes
½ cup chopped green sweet pepper
¼ cup grated Parmesan cheese

⅓ cup bread crumbs
Salt and pepper to taste
6 sprigs parsley

Fry bacon until evenly browned. Drain, crumble, and set aside. Slice off stem ends of each tomato. Gently scoop out pulp, leaving a ½-inch wall. Finely chop pulp; place ⅓ cup pulp in medium bowl. Discard remaining pulp. Stir crumbled bacon, green pepper, cheese, bread crumbs and salt and pepper into tomato pulp. Spoon into hollowed-out tomatoes. Place stuffed tomatoes into greased 7x11-inch baking dish and bake at 350 degrees for 20 to 25 minutes. Garnish with parsley sprigs.

Todd Collins

For a refined palate like Todd's, this simple dish touches on every note. The tang of the bell pepper is a perfect complement to the fat of the bacon.

CHICKEN ROLL-UPS

2 large boneless, skinless chicken
    breasts
1 can cream of chicken soup
6 ounces chicken broth
6 ounces milk

1 tablespoon flour
Salt and pepper to taste
1 can crescent rolls
6 ounces shredded cheddar cheese

Boil chicken until tender. Remove chicken, but save broth. Shred chicken and set aside. Whisk together soup, broth, milk, flour, salt, and pepper. Unroll crescent dough. Separate into triangles. Place a little cheese over dough (reserve some to sprinkle over roll-ups after baking), and at larger end place a good heaping of cooked chicken. Roll up and place in 9x13-inch casserole dish. Repeat until you have used all of the crescent rolls. Once all are in dish, pour soup mix around each and then drizzle some over tops. Bake at 375 degrees for 25 minutes. Remove. Add more cheese on top and return to oven for 5 minutes. Let sit for a couple of minutes before serving. The soup mixture will thicken up like gravy. Makes 8 rolls.

Kassidy McGuire
*Kassidy enjoys working alongside her
mom to make these tasty roll-ups.*

CHICKEN AND NOODLES

3 egg yolks
1 whole egg
3 tablespoons cold water
1 teaspoon salt

2 cups flour
Chicken broth
Chicken, cooked and diced

Beat egg yolks and whole egg together. Beat in cold water and salt. Stir in flour, then knead. Divide into three parts and roll thin. Cut into thin strips and dry on floured cloth before cooking.

To cook: In pot, bring chicken broth to a boil. Add chicken and noodles and cook until noodles are tender (8 to 12 minutes).

CHICKEN IN A CRUMB BASKET

CRUMB BASKET:

½ cup melted butter
6 cups bread crumbs
¼ cup chopped onion

1 teaspoon celery salt
½ teaspoon poultry seasoning

Mix all ingredients in bowl. Line bottom and sides of greased 2-quart casserole dish with mixture, forming a "basket." Bake at 350 degrees for 15 minutes.

FILLING:

¼ cup butter
¼ cup flour
½ cup milk
1½ cups chicken broth

1 cup finely chopped carrot
1 cup finely chopped potato
3 cups finely chopped cooked chicken
1 cup fresh or frozen peas

Make white sauce by melting butter, browning flour in the butter, then slowly adding milk, followed by broth. In separate pot, cook carrots and potatoes in water until soft. Drain. Add chicken and peas. Coat with white sauce. Pour into crumb basket and bake at 350 degrees for 30 to 40 minutes.

Heidi Troyer

Heidi particularly enjoyed teaching her students how to make this delectable dish (one of her personal favorites, passed down from several generations of women in her family).

CREAMY DRIED BEEF AND CABBAGE

½ large head cabbage, chopped	1½ cups white sauce
¼ pound dried beef	½ cup buttered bread crumbs

Cook cabbage in salted water until tender. Drain. Chop dried beef and soak in warm water for 10 minutes; drain. Place alternating layers of cabbage and dried beef into greased casserole dish. Pour white sauce on top, then add bread crumbs. Bake at 350 degrees for 25 minutes.

Eli Miller

For the single man, trying to make his way around the kitchen on his own, this is the perfect dish. Eli Miller highly recommends it.

GERMAN PIZZA

1 pound ground beef, browned	2 tablespoons butter
½ half medium onion, chopped	6 raw potatoes, shredded
½ green pepper, diced	3 eggs, beaten
1½ teaspoon salt, divided	⅓ cup milk
½ teaspoon pepper	2 cups shredded cheddar or mozzarella cheese

In 12-inch skillet, brown beef with onion, green pepper, ½ teaspoon salt, and pepper. Remove beef mixture from skillet; drain skillet and melt butter. Spread potatoes over butter and sprinkle with remaining 1 teaspoon salt. Top with beef mixture. Combine eggs and milk, and pour over all. Cook, covered on medium heat until potatoes are tender, about 30 minutes. Top with cheese, cover and heat until cheese melts, about 5 minutes. Cut into wedges or squares to serve.

Heidi Troyer

Goulash

2 pounds ground beef
1½ cups chopped onion
1 green sweet pepper, chopped
1 clove garlic, minced
2 cups macaroni, cooked and drained
2 to 3 tablespoons chili powder

Salt and pepper to taste
½ teaspoon garlic powder
2 (16 ounce) cans chili beans
2 (14.5 ounce) cans diced tomatoes
2 to 3 cups tomato juice

Cook ground beef, onion, pepper, and garlic in skillet. Drain. Pour into stockpot and add remaining ingredients. Cook over low heat, allowing to simmer for 20 to 30 minutes until all flavors combine.

Lance Freemont

The perfect "guy meal." Guaranteed to fill your belly and keep you going on those days when you've got a lot of work to do.

Ground Beef Casserole

2 pounds lean ground beef	Salt and pepper to taste
1 small onion, diced	8 ounces noodles
½ cup chopped green sweet pepper	1 (8 ounce) package cream cheese
1 clove garlic, crushed	8 ounces sour cream
1 (15 ounce) can tomato sauce	Parmesan cheese

Brown ground beef, then drain and add onion and green pepper. Cook until onion is tender. Add garlic, tomato sauce, and salt and pepper to taste. Simmer for 15 minutes. Cook noodles. Beat cream cheese and sour cream together until smooth. Layer noodles, cheese, and meat sauce in buttered casserole dish, then sprinkle with Parmesan cheese. Bake at 350 degrees until sides bubble, 20 to 30 minutes.

Lisa Brooks

Some might argue that Lisa's culinary tastes aren't as refined as one might expect from a caterer/chef, but she aims to please with this tasty and filling dish.

HAM AND CHEESE STICKY BUNS

1 (12 count) package whole wheat
    dinner rolls
½ pound sliced ham
1 pound Swiss cheese
¼ cup butter

2 tablespoons Worcestershire sauce
2 tablespoons poppy seeds
2 tablespoons prepared mustard
⅓ cup brown sugar

Remove dinner rolls from package without breaking apart individual rolls. Slice whole group of rolls in half and set bottom half in greased 9x13-inch pan. Layer with ham and cheese. Cover with top layer of rolls. In saucepan, combine butter, Worcestershire sauce, poppy seeds, mustard, and brown sugar until dissolved into a sauce. Pour over and between rolls. Bake uncovered at 350 degrees for 10 minutes. Cover with foil and bake 10 more minutes. Slice apart and serve.

ARLENE T. MILLER, *Sugarcreek, OH*

HAM WITH RAISIN SAUCE

1 tablespoon butter
1 tablespoon flour
1 cup water
¼ cup brown sugar

¼ teaspoon salt
3 tablespoons lemon juice
½ cup raisins
6 thick (approximately 1 inch) slices
    ham

Melt butter in saucepan. Stir in flour, then add water and bring to a boil. Add brown sugar, salt, and lemon juice and allow to heat. Stir in raisins and simmer until mixture thickens. Place ham slices in lightly greased casserole dish. Pour raisin sauce on top, then cover with foil and bake at 325 degrees for 45 minutes.

Ron Hensley

Ron loves a good ham, but even he was surprised just how much he loves this recipe using raisin sauce.

Heidi's Sweet and Sour Meat Loaf

1½ pounds ground beef
1 medium onion, chopped
1 cup saltine cracker crumbs

1 teaspoon pepper
1½ teaspoons salt
1 egg, beaten

In mixing bowl, combine ground beef and onion. Add cracker crumbs, pepper, salt, and egg. Mix well. Shape into loaf and place in 9x5-inch loaf pan.

Topping:

½ cup tomato sauce
1 cup water
2 tablespoons cider vinegar

2 tablespoons prepared mustard
2 tablespoons brown sugar

In mixing bowl, combine all ingredients. Spread over meat. Bake at 350 degrees for 1½ hours.

Heidi Troyer

A new twist on an old favorite. Heidi is happy to pass along this family recipe.

Lyle's Favorite Braised Beef Liver

1 pound beef liver
1 cup milk
3 tablespoons flour
½ teaspoon salt
4 tablespoons oil or bacon grease

1 onion, sliced
2 cups beef broth
2 tablespoons lemon juice
1 tablespoon sugar
¼ cup sour cream

Cut liver into 1-inch strips, then soak in milk. After 1 hour, remove liver and dredge in mixture of flour and salt. Sauté liver in hot oil until browned on all sides. Remove and set aside to drain. Brown onion in same pan. Remove and place on top of liver. Add beef broth, lemon juice, and sugar to hot pan and deglaze. Place liver and onion back into pan and warm for 5 minutes. Turn off heat and add sour cream.

Heidi Troyer

This dish will most assuredly change the minds of those who are dubious about beef liver. It won over Heidi's husband, Lyle, in short order.

Dumplings

1 egg, beaten
½ cup milk
1¼ stick butter, melted and cooled
1 teaspoon salt

3 cups flour
Chicken broth
Salt and pepper to taste

Stir together egg, milk, butter, and salt; add flour, then chill. Roll thin and slice into strips. Boil in chicken broth, adding salt and pepper to taste.

Meatballs

1 pound ground beef
1 large egg
¼ cup finely chopped onion
⅓ cup old-fashioned oats
¼ cup milk

1 teaspoon Worcestershire sauce
⅛ teaspoon salt
⅛ teaspoon pepper
1 cup ketchup or tomato sauce

Grease a 9x13-inch baking dish and set aside. Mix the ground beef, egg, onion, oats, milk, Worcestershire sauce, salt, and pepper in a bowl. Then shape the mixture by tablespoonful into 1½-inch balls. Place the meatballs in the prepared baking dish. Pour ketchup over the meatballs, and bake at 400 degrees for 20 to 25 minutes. Makes about 25 meatballs, depending on size.

Heidi Troyer

Sauerbraten

Chuck or pot roast (2 to 3 pounds, approximately 2 inches thick)
Vinegar
Water

2 large onions, sliced
4 slices bacon
1 tablespoon whole cloves
1 teaspoon whole allspice

Gravy:

1 to 2 tablespoons cornstarch
¼ cup water

1 tablespoon sugar

Place meat in dish or bowl and cover with solution of half vinegar and half water; add sliced onion. Refrigerate. Do this two days before meat is wanted. On the day before it is to be cooked, cut bacon into 1-inch pieces. Take some of the onion that has been soaking in the vinegar and chop finely to equal 1 tablespoon. Cut holes in meat every inch or so and stuff bits of bacon and chopped onion into holes. Put meat back into solution; add cloves and allspice. Refrigerate until the next day. In a greased skillet, sear both sides of roast. Transfer to an oven-safe dish with part of the marinating solution; cover. Bake at 325 degrees for 3 to 4 hours or in a Crock-Pot on low for 6 hours, until tender. Remove beef to platter and slice. Strain solids from remaining broth. Cook liquid over medium heat. Mix cornstarch with water and add to broth to thicken to desired consistency, then add sugar. This will form a dark gravy, which should be served over the roast.

Oven Fried Chicken

1 (3 pound) whole fryer	1 cup flour
½ cup butter or margarine	1 teaspoon baking powder
1 egg	2 teaspoons paprika
½ cup evaporated milk	1 teaspoon salt

Cut up fryer into serving pieces; pat dry. Preheat oven to 400 degrees and melt butter on cookie sheet. In shallow bowl, beat eggs and milk. In another shallow bowl, mix flour, baking powder, paprika, and salt. Dip chicken into egg mixture then roll in dry mixture. Place chicken skin side down on buttered pan. Bake at 400 degrees for 30 minutes. Turn over chicken and bake 30 more minutes.

AARON C. A. SCHWARTZ, *Galesburg, KS*

Sloppy Sandwiches

1 pound ground beef	1 (10 ounce) can cream soup
½ small onion, chopped	(chicken, mushroom, or celery)
½ teaspoon garlic, minced	12 hamburger buns

Brown ground beef, onion, and garlic. Add soup and simmer until thickened. Serve on buns or bread.

Bill Mason

A simple meal to fill up the guys at the hunting cabin.

Mock Steak Patties

1½ pounds ground beef	½ teaspoon pepper
1½ cups crushed saltine crackers	1 can cream of mushroom soup
¾ cup milk	¾ can water
1½ teaspoons salt	

Mix together ground beef, crackers, milk, salt, and pepper. Chill. Form into patties and fry. Layer patties in roaster pan. Combine soup and water. Pour over and between patties. Bake at 350 degrees for about 45 minutes or until done.

KATIE ZOOK, *Apple Creek, OH*

Swiss Steak

2 pounds round steak
½ cup flour
¼ cup oil

1 small onion, sliced
1 pint tomato juice
1 teaspoon salt

Pound meat, then dredge in flour. Put oil in skillet and heat. Brown steak on both sides. Add onion, tomato juice, and salt. Simmer 2 hours.

Trent Cooper

Trent enjoys helping his wife make this steak and including baked potatoes with the meal.

Sweet 'n' Smoky Chicken

1 large onion, sliced
4 chicken leg quarters
1 teaspoon salt
¼ teaspoon pepper
½ cup ketchup

2 tablespoons yellow mustard
¼ cup vinegar
½ cup maple syrup
½ teaspoon liquid smoke (optional)

Place onion slices in bottom of shallow pan. Place chicken in single layer, skin side up, on top of onion. Sprinkle with salt and pepper. Combine remaining ingredients and pour over chicken. Bake uncovered at 350 degrees for 1 hour or until done. Baste often with juices.

Katie Burkholder, *Middlefield, OH*

Hunter's No-Peek Stew

1½ pounds stew meat, cut fine
1 onion, chopped
6 carrots, diced
2 potatoes, cubed
1 teaspoon sugar

1 stalk celery, thickly sliced
2 cups tomato juice
2 teaspoons salt
2½ teaspoons Minute Tapioca

Preheat oven to 250 degrees. Place all ingredients in oven-safe casserole dish. Cover tightly. Bake for 4 hours.

Bill Mason

Perfect for during or after the big hunt.

Taco Bake

2 pounds ground beef
½ package taco seasoning
4 eggs
¾ cup milk
1 cup flour
1 teaspoon baking powder
½ teaspoon salt
1 (10 ounce) can cream of mushroom
soup
3 cups chopped lettuce
½ cup chopped green onions
½ cup chopped green pepper
2 cups shredded cheese

In skillet, brown beef; drain. Add taco seasoning. Spoon into greased 9x13-inch baking dish. In bowl, beat eggs and milk. Add flour, baking powder, and salt. Pour over meat. Bake uncovered at 400 degrees for 20 to 25 minutes or until golden brown. Spread mushroom soup on top. Top with lettuce, onions, peppers, and cheese.

TINA EICHER, *Hudson, KY*

WHEN-THE-BISHOP-CALLS CASSEROLE

2 boneless chicken breasts

3 cups water

2 tablespoons chopped celery

1 tablespoon chopped parsley

1 pinch salt

1 pinch pepper

8 ounces wide egg noodles

½ cup butter

8 ounces button mushrooms, stems removed and caps sliced

½ cup flour

¼ teaspoon ground sage (or to taste)

1 cup milk

⅓ cup freshly grated Parmesan cheese

Place chicken into saucepan and cover with water; add celery, parsley, salt, and pepper. Bring to a boil, then lower to a simmer and cook for 20 minutes. Remove chicken to cutting board and chop into inch-long pieces. Strain liquid into measuring cup; you will need 2 cups, so discard some or add water as necessary to attain that amount. Bring large pot of water to a boil and cook noodles, then drain. Melt butter in skillet over medium heat, then sauté mushrooms until they begin to brown. Sprinkle with flour and sage and continue to cook for 2 minutes, stirring occasionally. Add measured broth and milk. Use whisk to stir together over medium-low heat for about 5 minutes until mixture is thick and smooth. Combine drained noodles with sauce. Add chicken and toss well. Place in greased 3-quart casserole dish and sprinkle with cheese. Bake at 350 degrees about 30 minutes, until casserole is heated through and bubbling and top is lightly browned.

Heidi Trozer

Heidi doesn't save this recipe for the bishop's visits.
She serves it to Lyle on a regular basis.

Tuna Melt

2 (7 ounce) cans tuna in water,
  drained and flaked
¼ cup finely chopped green pepper
1 tablespoon onion, grated
6 tablespoons mayonnaise
1 teaspoon Dijon mustard

4 teaspoons Worcestershire sauce
¼ teaspoon pepper
4 English muffins, split, or 8 slices
  whole wheat bread
8 ounces cheddar cheese, thinly sliced

In a mixing bowl, combine tuna, green pepper, onion, mayonnaise, mustard, Worcestershire sauce, and pepper. Toast muffins and spread the mixture onto the 8 muffin halves. Top with slices of cheese. Broil 4 inches from the heat for 3 minutes, or until the cheese melts and browns lightly.

Miranda Cooper
A quick and inexpensive family meal.

Wigglers

3 pounds ground beef
3 onions, chopped
3 cups chopped potato
3 cups chopped celery
3 cups chopped carrot

3 cups peas
3 cups cooked spaghetti
1 quart tomatoes
2 cans cream of mushroom soup
1 pound grated cheese

Cook ground beef and onions in skillet. Mix chopped potato, celery, and carrot together with peas, spaghetti, and meat. Put in large roasting pan. Puree tomatoes and blend with soup. Pour tomato mixture over top of other ingredients. Cover with cheese and bake at 350 degrees for 1 hour.

Nichole Smith
Nichole finally figured out a way to get her siblings to eat vegetables once Heidi passed down this recipe. What kid could resist a meal with such a name?

Amish: Slow and Steady Wins the Race

You see them everywhere—people racing from place to place, cell phones in hand. They barely make it to the subway door, then do business by phone the whole time they're onboard. They carry on work-related transactions at the kids' T-ball game and pay bills during their lunch break. They swallow down meals from fast-food restaurants while still in the car. Rarely do you see these folks slowing down, unless they're forced to.

The Amish approach things differently. They work hard—in many ways harder than most. They are physically active all day long. But when it comes to the overall pace of their lives, they are not in a hurry. A slow buggy ride to town? No problem. A leisurely visit on a neighbor's porch? Of course. A full afternoon teaching the children how to garden or sew? Pure delight. No rushing necessary.

There's something to be said for slowing down, pausing to take in the beauty of nature, to revel in the softness of a newborn baby's skin, to enjoy a lingering conversation with a loved one without the constant interruption of text messages or phone calls.

For the Amish, quiet and steady go hand in hand. They understand the seasons and know that crops take time to grow. All good things come in their ordained time. This is even true in the Amish kitchen. The Amish cook isn't popping things into a microwave, hoping for instant (but bland) results. She's taking her time—prepping, stirring, greasing the pan, firing up the wood (or gas) stove. She's kneading dough, knowing that it will take time to rise. She's canning peaches, knowing they won't be eaten for weeks, or possibly months. She's stirring a pot of soup, enjoying the mixture of aromas as it simmers while she goes about her daily work.

In short, she's enjoying the process as much as the outcome. And when a lovely outcome is the goal, it's worth the extra time. Isn't this just what our heavenly Father teaches us in His Word? He makes everything beautiful. . .in His time.

RECIPES FOR SOUPS

———— ✦ ————

To every thing there is a season,
and a time to every purpose
under the heaven.

ECCLESIASTES 3:1

———— ✦ ————

Cheesy Chicken Chowder

2 cups diced potato
1 cup diced celery
1 cup diced carrot
½ cup chopped onion
¼ cup butter
⅓ cup flour

1½ teaspoons salt
¼ teaspoon pepper
3 cups chicken broth
2 cups milk
2 cups shredded cheese
2 cups chopped cooked chicken

In pot, boil vegetables in water until tender. In large pot, melt butter; add flour, salt, and pepper. Stir until bubbly. Add broth and milk; boil until thickened. Add cheese and chicken. Bring to a boil. Add vegetables and mix in. Simmer a few minutes.

Martha Petersheim, Verdigre, NE

Bacon and Split Pea Soup

1 pound bacon
1 large onion, diced
2 large carrots, diced
3 cloves garlic, minced

Salt and pepper to taste
4 cups low-sodium chicken broth
12 ounces split peas, rinsed
Chopped parsley

Cook bacon in large saucepan until crispy, transfer to paper towel–lined plate and let cool, then crumble. Add onion, carrots, and garlic to remaining bacon fat in saucepan and cook until tender and golden, 6 to 8 minutes. Season generously with salt and pepper. Add broth and split peas and let simmer covered until split peas are tender, 35 to 40 minutes. Garnish with parsley and bacon.

Velma Kimball
*The addition of bacon in this recipe
makes it one of Velma's favorites.*

AMISH CORN CHOWDER

4 slices bacon
2 tablespoons diced onion
1 tablespoon diced celery
1 tablespoon diced sweet pepper
2 cups corn

2 potatoes, diced
3 tomatoes, chopped
Salt and pepper to taste
2 quarts (8 cups) milk
Chopped parsley

Dice bacon and put into pan to brown; add onion, celery, and pepper; fry until bacon is crisp. Add corn and fry together for 3 minutes. Add potatoes and tomatoes and season with salt and pepper. Cover and simmer for 30 minutes. Add milk, heat to boiling, then remove from heat. Top with chopped parsley.

Darren Keller

According to Darren, this is a guy's perfect comfort food.

CHICKEN AND RICE SOUP

3 boneless, skinless chicken breasts	½ cup chopped carrots
2 tablespoons oil	3 chicken bouillon cubes (or granules)
8 cups water	¾ cup rice (white or brown)
1 small onion, chopped	3 tablespoons flour
1 cup chopped celery	

Fry chicken breasts in oil, then dice into pieces of desired size. Place in cooking pot with water, onions, celery, carrots, and bouillon. Cook until vegetables are nearly tender, then add rice. Cook 20 to 30 minutes or until rice is tender. If necessary, thicken with flour until soup reaches desired consistency.

Allie Garrett

This is a go-to meal for Allie when she's busy with the kids.

CREAM OF CELERY SOUP

1 stick butter	½ teaspoon celery seed
3 cups finely chopped celery	Salt and pepper to taste
½ cup diced onion	3 tablespoons cornstarch
4 cups chicken broth	3 tablespoons water
3 cups milk	

Melt butter in saucepan and sauté celery and onion. Add chicken broth and bring to a boil. Simmer 15 minutes. Add milk and seasonings. Warm. Thicken with cornstarch dissolved in water.

DUTCH COUNTRY BEAN SOUP

1 pound soup beans	½ cup diced potato
1 ham bone	1 (15 ounce) can tomato sauce
½ cup chopped onion	2 teaspoons minced parsley
1 cup diced celery	Salt and pepper to taste

Soak beans in water overnight. Drain; add fresh water and cook slowly with ham bone for 2 hours. Add remaining ingredients. Simmer until vegetables are soft. Remove ham bone, trim off any meat, cut it up, and add to soup. For additional texture and flavor, chop a couple of hard-boiled eggs and add them to soup.

Friendship Soup

½ cup dry split peas

⅓ cup beef bouillon granules

¼ cup pearl barley

½ cup dry lentils

¼ cup onion flakes

2 teaspoons dried Italian seasoning

½ cup uncooked long-grain white rice

2 bay leaves

½ cup uncooked alphabet pasta

In 1½-pint jar, layer split peas, bouillon, barley, lentils, onion flakes, Italian seasoning, rice, and bay leaves. Wrap uncooked pasta in plastic wrap and place in jar. Seal tightly. Attach label to jar with written instructions:

Friendship Soup

ADDITIONAL INGREDIENTS:

1 pound ground beef

Black pepper to taste

Garlic powder to taste

1 (28 ounce) can diced tomatoes, undrained

1 (6 ounce) can tomato paste

3 quarts water

TO PREPARE SOUP: Remove pasta from top of jar and set aside. In large pot over medium heat, brown beef with pepper and garlic; drain excess fat. Add diced tomatoes, tomato paste, water, and soup mix. Bring to a boil, then reduce heat to low. Cover and simmer for 45 minutes. Stir in pasta, cover, and simmer 15 to 20 minutes or until pasta, peas, lentils, and barley are tender.

Denise and Kassidy McGuire

Inspired by cooking class, mother and daughter made jars of this soup starter for Christmas gifts for family and clients.

Potato Ham Soup

1½ cups cubed potato
4 tablespoons butter
3 tablespoons flour
1 cup chopped ham

2 teaspoons chicken base
1 cup water
1 cup milk

Boil potatoes in water until soft; drain. Melt butter in pot. Add flour and stir until smooth and bubbly. Add potatoes, ham, chicken base, and 1 cup water. Stir occasionally until soup comes to a boil. Add milk. Stir to warm and thicken.

Mattie Yoder, *Fairchild, WI*

White Bean Chicken Chili Soup

2 pounds cooked chicken, diced
1 (48 ounce) jar great northern
  beans, undrained
12 ounces shredded pepper jack
  cheese

2 teaspoons cumin
1 (46 ounce) can chicken broth
1 can green chilies (optional)

Combine all ingredients and cook slowly over low heat. Cheese will be less stringy when added to cold ingredients. Serve with sour cream and tortilla chips.

Mary Yoder, *Millersburg, OH*

SPAETZLE (AMISH DUMPLINGS)

1 cup milk
2 cups flour
2 eggs

1 teaspoon salt
Water or broth

Slowly add milk to flour. Stir constantly to keep mixture smooth. Add 1 egg at a time, beating well after each. Salt and mix well. Cook in boiling salted water or meat broth, pouring batter from shallow bowl, tilting it over boiling pot. Use sharp knife to slice off pieces of batter into boiling liquid. Dip knife in liquid before each cut to prevent sticking.

Jeremy Keller

The boy was fascinated to watch Heidi teach about these dumplings, and now he and his dad have perfected them at home.

Potato Rivvel Soup

5 potatoes	1 to 1½ quarts milk
1 medium onion	½ cup butter
Salt and pepper to taste	2 eggs
8 cups water	Flour

Boil potatoes, onion, salt, and pepper in water until potatoes are nearly soft. Drain off most of water and replace with milk, then heat. Add butter. In separate bowl, make rivvels: Whisk eggs and add flour until you can form lumpy balls about the size of grapes. Sift out excess flour. Drop rivvels into hot potato-milk mixture and boil for 15 minutes. Use care not to scald milk.

Charlene Higgins

When it comes to cooking, Charlene likes to keep it simple. That's why she's crazy about this easy-to-make soup.

Sauerkraut Soup

1 pound smoked Polish sausage, cut into ½-inch pieces	3 (14.5 ounce) cans chicken broth
5 medium potatoes, peeled and cubed	1 (32 ounce) can sauerkraut, rinsed and drained
2 medium onions, chopped	1 (6 ounce) can tomato paste
2 carrots, cut into ¼-inch slices	

Combine sausage, potatoes, onions, carrots, and chicken broth in large saucepan; bring to a boil. Reduce heat; cover and simmer for 30 minutes or until potatoes are almost tender. Don't let them overcook. Add sauerkraut and tomato paste; mix well. Return to a boil. Reduce heat; cover and simmer 30 minutes longer.

Velma Kimball

Velma just can't say no to sauerkraut, even in soup form.

Amish Skill Sharing

Life gives us many opportunities to compete with those around us. It starts when we're kids in school and continues into adulthood, when we're climbing the corporate ladder. Whether it's sports, grades, or vying for that cute boy's attention, we're always trying to one-up the next person. A little competition never hurt anyone, right? Perhaps not, but when we're always looking out for number one, when we're set on coming out on top, we're rarely others-focused.

The Amish have a completely different outlook. They are intent on sharing their skills, their know-how, with others. Men within each district help one another with construction projects, furniture crafting, or farming techniques while women work together on crafts like card-making, stitching beautiful quilts, or sharing tasty foods. Recipes are freely passed from friend to friend, home to home, as are age-old cooking tips.

Why share so freely? Why don't these ladies hold their recipes close when complimented for a yummy pie or tasty cake? Why not bask in the pride and joy of being told they're better than the rest? Because they are not. And the Amish recognize that God's heart, God's way, involves letting go of pride.

There is a tremendous amount of joy in sharing skills with a loved one or a new friend in the community. How fun the Amish kitchen must be, when friends gather together to learn to make jams and jellies or to prepare beef jerky. What joy to teach a new mama how to feed that little one nutritious baby foods, made from scratch. And what a great satisfaction to be able to pass on the legacy of cooking dumplings or shoofly pie to your children and grandchildren.

The Amish kitchen is a school, in and of itself. And what a fun school it must be!

MISCELLANEOUS RECIPES

❦

Iron sharpeneth iron;
so a man sharpeneth the
countenance of his friend.

PROVERBS 27:17

❦

Canine Treats

⸎

Chicken and Rice Dog Biscuits

6 ounces boneless chicken breast,
  boiled
½ cup cooked wild rice
½ cup chicken broth

2½ cups all-purpose or wheat flour
¼ teaspoon salt
1 egg

Combine chicken, rice, and stock in food processor or blender and pulse until it becomes a paste. Combine flour, salt, egg, and chicken paste in bowl; mix well. Sprinkle a little flour on flat surface and knead dough until it is no longer sticky, then roll it out with rolling pin about ½-inch thick. Cut out shapes and place them on baking sheet lined with parchment paper. Bake at 350 degrees for 25 to 30 minutes until light brown.

Allie Garrett and Her Children
Perfect choice for that new family pup!

Veggie Dog Treats

1 cup pumpkin puree
¼ cup peanut butter
2 large eggs
½ cup old-fashioned oats

3 cups whole wheat flour
1 carrot, peeled and shredded
1 zucchini, shredded
1 cup baby spinach, chopped

Beat pumpkin puree, peanut butter, and eggs on medium-high until well combined, about 1 to 2 minutes. Slowly add oats and flour at low speed. Beat until incorporated. If necessary, add additional flour until dough is not sticky. Add carrot, zucchini, and spinach, beating just until incorporated. Working on lightly floured surface, knead dough until it comes together. Roll dough to ¼-inch thickness. Using cookie cutters, cut out desired small shapes and place on baking sheet lined with parchment paper. Place into oven and bake at 350 degrees until edges are golden brown, about 20 to 25 minutes. Let cool completely.

Rusty's Pumpkin Dog Biscuits

2 eggs
½ cup canned pumpkin
½ teaspoon salt

2 tablespoons dry milk
2½ cups flour
Water

Blend eggs and pumpkin together. Add salt, dry milk, and flour. Add enough water to make dough workable. It should be dry and stiff. Don't worry about crumbs remaining in bowl. Dough will be too stiff for electric mixer, so work it with your hands. Roll to ½-inch thick. Cut into shapes. Place 1 inch apart on ungreased baking sheet and bake at 350 degrees for 20 minutes on one side, then turn over and bake another 20 minutes.

Heidi Trozer

Heidi and Lyle's dog, Rusty, would like to offer a paw of praise to his owner Heidi for making these delectable pumpkin dog biscuits. They're his personal favorites (and not just at Christmastime).

Health

Lavender Bath Spa Salts

2 cups Epsom salt
½ cup baking soda

10 to 15 drops lavender essential oil
Purple food coloring

Combine salt, soda, and oil in a stainless steel bowl, rubbing together with hands until very well combined. Add food coloring to create desired shade of lavender. Package in small clear cellophane bags and tie with ribbons. To use: Add desired amount to your bath water and dissolve.

Variations:

- Use rose essential oil and tint the bath salts pink.
- Use jasmine essential oil and tint the bath salts yellow.
- Use eucalyptus essential oil and tint the bath salts pale green.

Kathryn Troyer, *Rutherford, TN*

Lavender Lotion

⅓ cup coconut oil
1 tablespoon beeswax

5 drops lavender essential oil

Using double boiler, melt coconut oil and beeswax together, then add essential oil. Cool and store in sealed container. Lavender is perfect for calming yourself. Use on hands, feet, and legs to help you sleep.

Peggy Ann Kimball
A simple gift a girl can make for her family.

Lip Balm/Salve

2 tablespoons beeswax

2 tablespoons shea butter

2 tablespoons coconut oil

8 to 10 drops peppermint essential oil

12 to 14 lip balm tubes

Melt beeswax, shea butter, and coconut oil in double boiler, stirring constantly until melted. Remove pan from heat but keep over the still-hot water to keep mixture melted. Add essential oil, a few drops at a time. Use dropper to fill lip balm tubes. Work quickly because mixture will begin to harden fast. Let tubes sit at room temperature for several hours until cooled and completely hardened before capping them.

Nichole Smith

Every teen girl needs the perfect lip balm, especially in the winter. Nichole is happy to share this recipe with friends of all ages.

Shaving Soap

¼ cup natural aloe vera gel (not juice)

¼ cup liquid castile soap

1 tablespoon almond oil

¼ cup warm distilled water

1 teaspoon vitamin E or grapefruit seed extract

8 to 10 drops lavender essential oil

8 ounce or larger foaming soap bottle

Combine ingredients in foamer bottle and shake gently until mixed. Shake well before each use.

Ron Hensley

Ron is happy to pass along his personal recipe for shaving soap.

Household

Homemade All-Purpose Cleaner

¼ to ½ cup vinegar

2 tablespoons baking soda

8 to 10 drops tea tree or eucalyptus
essential oil

Enough water to fill bottle

Pour vinegar in spray bottle and add baking soda. Add a few drops of your favorite essential oil and then fill bottle to the top with water.

Loretta Donnelly

*As an Englisher, Loretta never made her own cleaners.
As an Amish woman, she's excited to learn new recipes
like this one, passed to her from the bishop's wife.*

Wood Polishing Spray

¼ cup olive oil

¼ cup vinegar

10 drops orange or lemon essential oil

Add olive oil and vinegar to glass spray bottle. Add essential oil. Shake before each use. Apply to cloth and wipe surfaces clean.

Eli Miller

Eli uses this mixture in his workshop.

Homemade Glass Cleaner

¼ cup rubbing alcohol

¼ cup vinegar

1 tablespoon cornstarch

2 cups warm water

Combine all ingredients in spray bottle and shake well. Before each use, shake again (as cornstarch might settle at bottom and plug spray mechanism).

Lance Freemont

Lance likes to keep the windows in his home clean and found this recipe works great.

Dish Soap

1 tablespoon borax

1 tablespoon grated Ivory soap

1¾ cups boiling water

15 to 20 drops essential oil (your choice of scent)

Combine borax and grated Ivory soap in medium bowl. Pour boiling water over mixture. Whisk until Ivory soap is completely melted. Allow mixture to cool for 6 to 8 hours, stirring occasionally. Dish soap will eventually gel. Transfer to squirt bottle and add essential oils of your choice. Shake to combine.

Heidi Trozer

A family recipe, passed down from Heidi's grandmother.

Laundry Soap

1 bar Zote soap

1 cup washing soda

1 cup borax

20 drops essential oil (your choice of scent)

1 cup oxygen booster

Grate soap into fine particles using hand grater or food processor. Combine with washing soda and borax (using gloves). Add essential oils and stir. Store in airtight glass jar. Use 1 to 2 tablespoons per load.

Ellen Blackburn

Ellen loves the money this natural laundry soap saves her.

Amish Gardens

Amish gardens are not just a thing of beauty; they are a source of life for the Amish people. The task of tending God's land is one they take very seriously. In many ways, it is part of the fabric of their belief system. The wisdom they've passed down from generation to generation is remarkable. These amazing gardeners know what it means to care for the land in a natural way.

The first purpose of the gardens, of course, is to provide for the family. Nothing goes to waste. Whatever isn't eaten is sold or passed on to friends and loved ones. And speaking of passing things on, the Amish often exchange seedlings and plants with their neighbors. In this way, they maintain diverse plants in their gardens.

This method of "sharing the love" is indicative of their overall way of life. Nothing hoarded. Nothing wasted. All is produced for the greater good and to sustain life (and generate income) for the community.

As for when and how to plant, the Amish lean heavily on methods passed down from parents, grandparents, and so on. They plant according to the season and look for signs from nature itself. There is a lovely rhythm to the Amish gardening process, shifting from the warmth of spring to the heat of summer and then to crisp fall days.

Amish gardens aren't just practical though. They are lovely. As you drive through the Amish country, you can observe exquisite fields, producing a variety of colorful vegetables, flowers, and medicinal herbs. And where there are lovely gardens, there are insects in abundance—bees, butterflies, and other beneficial insects abound.

Gardening is an act of worship for the Amish. They cannot separate their spiritual lives from their work with the soil. In many ways, they feel they have been given a mandate from the Lord to care for the land He has given them (and they do a fine job). Crop growing also produces character, which is one reason you see Amish children working alongside their mothers and fathers. Weeding, watering, tending. . .Amish children know how to do it all. And so will their children, for the legacy of gardening is one passed down from generation to generation.

RECIPES FOR SALADS AND SIDES

And God blessed them, and God said unto them, Be fruitful, and multiply, and replenish the earth, and subdue it: and have dominion over the fish of the sea, and over the fowl of the air, and over every living thing that moveth upon the earth.

GENESIS 1:28

Amish Macaroni Salad

1 (12 ounce) box elbow macaroni
4 hard-boiled eggs
1 small red sweet pepper
1 small sweet onion
3 stalks celery
2 cups Miracle Whip dressing

2 tablespoons dill pickle relish
3 tablespoons yellow mustard
2 teaspoons vinegar
¼ cup sugar
¾ teaspoon celery seed

Boil pasta until tender. Rinse thoroughly, drain, and set aside. Chop eggs, pepper, onion, and celery. In large bowl, mix remaining ingredients and stir until incorporated. Pour vegetables and eggs on top of dressing; mix well. Add macaroni and stir until well blended. Place covered in refrigerator and chill before serving.

Bologna Salad

1½ pounds bologna, coarsely ground
½ cup finely diced celery
½ cup sweet pickle relish

1 tablespoon prepared mustard
½ to ¾ cup mayonnaise
Salt and pepper to taste

Combine all ingredients. Cover and chill until ready to serve. For additional flavor and texture, add 2 hard-boiled and chopped eggs.

Eli Miller

Easy. Practical. Tasty. Three words Eli uses to describe his new wife's bologna salad.

Caramel Apple Salad

1 small package instant butterscotch pudding
1 (8 ounce) tub whipped topping
1 (10 ounce) can crushed pineapple, including juice

1 cup miniature marshmallows
3 cups apples, pared and cut in small chunks

Mix all together; refrigerate for an hour before serving.

Jeremy Keller

Jeremy often asked for this salad, and he soon found it was easy to make.

Dump Salad

1 (16 to 24 ounce) can pineapple chunks
1 (15 ounce) can mandarin oranges
1 (24 ounce) tub large curd cottage cheese

1 (16 ounce) tub whipped topping
1 large package gelatin mix (orange, strawberry, or lime)

Drain canned fruit; discard juice. Empty cottage cheese into large bowl. Gradually add whipped topping. Stir in gelatin mix until well blended. Fold in drained fruit and chill at least 2 hours before serving.

SHIRLEY KUEPFER, *Newton, Ontario, Canada*

CHRISTMAS CRUNCH SALAD

4 cups broccoli, cut into small pieces
4 cups cauliflower, cut into small pieces
1 medium onion, chopped
8 cherry tomatoes, halved

Dressing:
1 cup mayonnaise
½ cup sour cream
1 to 2 tablespoons sugar
1 tablespoon cider vinegar
Salt and pepper to taste

Put cut vegetables in bowl. In another bowl, combine dressing ingredients. Pour over vegetables and toss well. Cover and chill in refrigerator for 1 to 2 hours.

Heidi Troyer

CONFETTI SALAD

1 cup chopped green sweet pepper
1 cup chopped onion
1 cup chopped celery
1 large pimiento, chopped

1 cup sauerkraut, drained
¾ cup sugar
1½ cups vinegar

Combine all ingredients for a festive, colorful salad.

Lisa Brooks

Lisa recently served this eye-catching dish at
•a wedding and the guests went back for seconds!

CRANBERRY SALAD

4 cups fresh ground cranberries
2 cups sugar
1 small bag miniature marshmallows

2 cups whipped cream
2 cups grapes or canned mandarin oranges
1 cup pecans or walnuts, chopped

Mix cranberries with sugar and marshmallows and let set overnight in refrigerator. Before serving, add remaining ingredients.

Becky Blackburn

Becky enjoyed making this during the holidays to share with family.

German Potato Salad

4 boiled potatoes, cut into chunks
1 teaspoon sugar
½ teaspoon salt
¼ teaspoon dry mustard
1 dash pepper

2 tablespoons cider vinegar
1 cup sour cream
½ cup thinly sliced onion
2 to 3 slices bacon, fried and cut
   into small pieces
Paprika

Place potato chunks in large bowl. Combine sugar, salt, dry mustard, pepper, vinegar, sour cream, onion, and bacon pieces. Pour over warm potatoes and toss lightly until coated with dressing. Serve warm with dash of paprika.

Heidi Troyer

A family recipe, passed down from Heidi's aunt. The addition of apple cider vinegar gives the dish a bit of a kick.

BROCCOLI BAKE

1 can cream of mushroom soup
1 cup mayonnaise
½ cup chopped onion
½ teaspoon salt
¼ teaspoon pepper

2 (10 ounce) packages frozen chopped
  broccoli, thawed
1 cup shredded sharp Cheddar cheese
1 (6 ounce) box herbed stuffing mix
¼ cup butter, melted and divided

In medium bowl, combine soup, mayonnaise, onion, salt, and pepper; mix well. Place half of broccoli in greased 3-quart casserole dish. Sprinkle with half of cheese and half of stuffing mix. Pour half of butter and half of soup mixture over stuffing. Repeat layers one more time. Bake at 350 degrees for 35 to 40 minutes or until hot in center.

Trent and Miranda Cooper
The couple worked together to learn to make this tasty dish the whole family enjoys.

Orange Dessert Salad

3 cups water
1 small package orange gelatin
1 small package instant vanilla
  pudding
1 small package tapioca pudding mix

1 (15 ounce) can mandarian oranges,
  drained
1 (8 ounce) can crushed pineapple,
  drained
1 (8 ounce) tub whipped topping

In large pan, boil water, then use whisk to stir in gelatin and pudding mixes. Return to a boil while stirring for 1 minute. Remove from stove and cool completely. Fold in fruit and whipped topping. Transfer to serving bowl and refrigerate for 2 hours. Makes 12 to 14 servings.

Loretta Donnelly
Her children ask for this often and
are learning to help make it.

Poppy Seed Dressing

1½ cups honey
2 teaspoons salt
2 teaspoons dry mustard
2 teaspoons onion flakes

⅔ cup vinegar
2 cups salad oil
3 tablespoons poppy seeds

Combine first five ingredients in quart jar, then add oil. Slowly add poppy seeds.

Lisa Brooks
Perfect for summer salads.
Easy to make, easy to store, easy to serve.

Baked Potato Pudding

1 cup diced bacon
1 onion, minced
4 potatoes, peeled and grated
4 eggs, beaten

1 cup milk
1 tablespoon diced parsley
Salt and pepper to taste

Sauté bacon and onion. Put grated potatoes in bowl and stir in bacon mixture, then add eggs, milk, parsley, and salt and pepper. Transfer to 1½-quart baking dish and bake at 375 degrees for 1 hour or until top is browned.

THREE BEAN BAKE

1 (16 ounce) can lima beans, drained
1 large can pork and beans, drained
1 (16 ounce) can kidney beans,
   drained
½ pound bacon, fried and crumbled;
   or chopped hot dogs; or ground
   beef, fried

2 medium onions, finely chopped
¾ cup brown sugar
¾ cup ketchup
1 tablespoon prepared mustard

Place beans, meat, and onions in Dutch oven. Mix brown sugar, ketchup, and mustard. Pour over beans and mix in. Bake at 275 degrees for 1 hour.

IVA TROYER, *Apple Creek, OH*

CREAMED CORN CASSEROLE

2 (14 to 16 ounce) cans creamed corn
3 (14 to 16 ounce) cans whole kernel
   corn, drained
1 sleeve saltine crackers, crushed
1 tablespoon sugar

Salt and pepper to taste
2 eggs
2 to 3 tablespoons butter, cut into
   slices
2 tablespoons real bacon bits or
   crumbled bacon

Combine corn, crackers, sugar, and salt and pepper in 3-quart casserole. Beat eggs and add to casserole. Stir well. Lay pats of butter evenly over casserole and sprinkle with bacon. Bake at 375 degrees for 1 hour plus 15 to 30 minutes. If corn starts drying too much on top, cover with foil to finish baking.

Charlene Higgins
Charlene is happy she didn't let
this easy recipe intimidate her.

CREAMED SPINACH

3 to 4 bunches spinach, trimmed	4 ounces cream cheese, cut into pieces
1 tablespoon butter	½ cup milk
2 teaspoons flour	1 dash pepper
½ teaspoon salt	⅛ teaspoon nutmeg

Wash spinach well. Sprinkle with salt and cook in saucepan until soft. Do not add water. Once spinach is tender, remove and chop very fine. Melt butter in saucepan. Add flour and ½ teaspoon salt to butter; mix. Slowly add cream cheese and milk, stirring constantly until mixture reaches thick consistency and cream cheese has melted. Combine mixture with chopped spinach. Add pepper and nutmeg and serve.

Ellen Blackburn

A great way to serve a healthy vegetable.

Dutch Cabbage Rolls

1 medium head cabbage (3 pounds)
½ pound ground beef
½ pound ground pork
1 (15 ounce) can tomato sauce, divided
1 small onion, chopped
½ cup uncooked long-grain rice
1 tablespoon dried parsley
½ teaspoon salt
½ teaspoon snipped fresh dill
⅛ teaspoon cayenne pepper
½ teaspoon sugar
1 (14.5 ounce) can diced tomatoes, undrained

Cook cabbage in boiling water until outer leaves pull away easily from head. Set aside 12 large leaves for rolls. In small bowl, combine beef, pork, ½ cup tomato sauce, onion, rice, parsley, salt, dill, and cayenne. Mix well. Cut out thick vein from bottom of each leaf, resulting in a V-shaped cut. Place about ¼ cup meat mixture on 1 cabbage leaf. Overlap cut ends of leaf. Fold in sides. Beginning from cut end, roll up. Repeat with each leaf. Slice remaining cabbage and place in ovenproof Dutch oven. Arrange cabbage rolls seam-side down over sliced cabbage. Combine remaining tomato sauce, sugar, and diced tomatoes; pour over rolls. Cover and bake at 350 degrees for 1½ hours or until cabbage rolls are tender.

Velma Kimball
This recipe is a crowd pleaser.

FRIED GREEN TOMATOES

4 green tomatoes
Flour for coating
3 tablespoons oil, divided
Salt and pepper to taste

2 tablespoons brown sugar
1 tablespoon flour
½ cup milk

Cut tomatoes into ½-inch slices. Dredge thickly with flour. Quick-fry slices in 2 tablespoons hot oil. Brown both sides thoroughly. Remove tomatoes and place on serving dish. Sprinkle with salt and pepper and brown sugar. Keep tomatoes warm. Add 1 tablespoon oil to pan drippings, then blend in 1 tablespoon flour. Add milk and cook mixture, stirring continuously. The resulting mixture should reach consistency of thick cream. Pour over tomatoes and serve.

HASH BROWNS

4 cups peeled, cooked, and shredded
    potato
2 tablespoons chopped onion
½ teaspoon salt

⅛ teaspoon pepper
2 tablespoons butter
2 tablespoons oil or bacon drippings

Toss potatoes with onion, salt, and pepper. Heat butter and oil in 10-inch skillet. Pack potato mixture into skillet, leaving ½-inch space around edge. Cook over low heat 10 to 15 minutes until bottom is brown. Turn and cook another 10 to 15 minutes. Tip: When preparing mashed potatoes for supper, we cook extra potatoes for this recipe. Just remove potatoes allotted for hash browns a little before thoroughly cooked tender. Shred when cool.

M. MILLER, *Wooster, OH*

HERB TOMATOES

6 ripe tomatoes, whole and peeled
⅔ cup salad oil
¼ cup vinegar
1 clove garlic, minced

¼ cup snipped parsley
¼ cup chopped green onion
Salt and pepper to taste
½ teaspoon thyme

Combine ingredients and marinate until tomatoes are flavored in spices.

Marinated Carrots

2 pounds carrots, sliced on an angle
1 can tomato soup
¾ cup vinegar
1 large onion, sliced
1 teaspoon salt

1 cup sugar
½ teaspoon pepper
1 teaspoon dry mustard
2 tablespoons oil
1 yellow sweet pepper, cut into strips

Cook carrots in water until almost done; drain. Mix remaining ingredients and add hot carrots. Cover and let marinate overnight. Will keep for at least two weeks in refrigerator. Serve cold, or heat and serve.

Mustard Beans

1 pound dry navy beans
1 cup brown sugar
4 tablespoons prepared mustard
½ teaspoon garlic powder
1 tablespoon liquid smoke

1 cup heavy cream
¼ pound bacon, fried
1 teaspoon salt
1 small onion, fried

Cook beans until done; drain. Add remaining ingredients. Bake 2 to 3 hours.

Martha Miller, *Edgar, WI*

Potato Casserole

6 medium potatoes, peeled and sliced
Salt and pepper to taste
1 sweet pepper, chopped
1 pimiento, diced
2 tablespoons butter

1 tablespoon flour
1 cup milk
8 ounces pepper jack cheese
8 ounces garlic cheese

Boil potatoes until just tender; drain. Place in 8x11-inch casserole dish. Salt and pepper potatoes. Sprinkle with peppers. In separate saucepan, melt butter. Add flour, then milk. When warmed, add both cheeses. Cook until melted and smooth. Pour over potatoes. Bake at 350 degrees for 45 to 60 minutes.

Ellen Blackburn

As a busy nurse, Ellen appreciates this easy recipe.

Roasted Brussels Sprouts

1 pound fresh brussels sprouts
3 tablespoons olive oil

Salt and pepper to taste
4 slices bacon

Clean sprouts and discard outer loose leaves. Cut in half. Place into plastic bag. Pour in olive oil; season with salt and pepper. Shake gently to coat. Pour sprouts onto rimmed baking sheet, spreading them out into one layer. Dice bacon and sprinkle over sprouts. Roast at 400 degrees for 30 to 35 minutes until golden brown, stirring every 10 minutes.

Lyle Troyer

Lyle adapted this one for the grill. Set the grill to medium-high heat (around 400 degrees). Make a large foil pouch to place sprouts and other ingredients in. Close pouch and place on grill for about 20 minutes.

SCALLOPED ASPARAGUS

3 tablespoons butter

3 tablespoons flour

2 (14 to 16 ounce) cans cut green
   asparagus

2 (12 ounce) cans evaporated milk

8 ounces shredded cheddar cheese

6 hard-boiled eggs, sliced

1 large bag potato chips

To make sauce, melt butter in saucepan and dissolve flour in it. Drain cans of asparagus and add liquid and evaporated milk to flour mixture, then stir in cheese. Spread asparagus spears in greased oblong baking dish and cover with sliced eggs. Crumble half of potato chips on top. Cover with cheese sauce and add more chips on top of that. Bake at 350 degrees for 20 minutes.

Todd Collins

Good enough to be served in the finest restaurants across America, yet simple enough for the home cook. Todd highly recommends this dish.

Sloppy Potatoes

3 medium potatoes, sliced
1 medium onion, sliced
1 tablespoon butter

½ teaspoon salt
½ cup water

In medium saucepan, bring all ingredients to a boil. Reduce to low and cook 15 minutes, stirring occasionally.

Lance Freemont

This is how his mother always cooked potatoes and how Lance still prefers them.

Sour Cream Potatoes

1 pint sour cream
1 tablespoon onion flakes
1 can cream of mushroom soup
9 cups cooked potato, shredded

1 cup shredded cheese
Salt and pepper to taste
2 tablespoons melted butter
½ cup cornflakes

Combine all ingredients except butter and cornflakes. Bake at 350 degrees for 1 hour. Mix butter and cornflakes together and add on top of potato mixture, then return to oven for 3 to 4 minutes, until slightly brown.

Tomato Pie

2 cups Bisquick
⅔ cup milk
6 tomatoes, peeled and sliced
½ teaspoon garlic salt

½ teaspoon basil leaves
½ teaspoon oregano
16 ounces Parmesan cheese, grated
1½ cups mayonnaise

Mix Bisquick and milk. Spread evenly in 10-inch pie plate. Layer with tomatoes, spices, and cheese. Repeat layers and spread mayonnaise on top, then top with another layer of cheese. Bake at 350 degrees for 30 minutes or until lightly browned.

Debbie Cooper

Sweet Potato Pudding

6 large sweet potatoes, peeled and
    quartered
½ cup butter, melted
⅔ cup dark brown sugar

⅔ cup sugar
4 eggs, beaten
⅔ cup orange juice
2 teaspoons vanilla

Boil potatoes in water until tender, about 20 minutes. Drain and mash. Combine mashed sweet potatoes with remaining ingredients in large mixing bowl. Stir until smooth. Pour into buttered 2½-quart baking dish and bake at 350 degrees for 40 minutes.

Todd Collins

*The secret to this culinary masterpiece is in the orange juice.
It adds just the right amount of tartness to the dish.
Even a food expert like Todd can't resist.*

Sweet and Sour Green Beans

3 slices bacon, chopped
1 cup chopped onion
1 tablespoon flour
¼ cup cider vinegar

2 (15 ounce) cans green beans,
    drained, liquid reserved
2 tablespoons sugar
1 teaspoon salt
¼ teaspoon pepper

Cook bacon until browned. Add onion and cook until translucent. Stir in flour and cook 2 minutes more. Pour vinegar and ¾ cup of reserved green bean liquid into pan. Add sugar, salt, and pepper. Stir to combine. Bring to a boil, reduce to a simmer, and stir in green beans. Continue cooking at a low simmer until beans are hot.

SQUASH CROQUETTES

2 cups finely chopped yellow squash
1 cup finely chopped onion
1 egg, beaten
1 teaspoon salt

1 teaspoon pepper
½ cup plus 1 tablespoon flour
Oil

In large bowl, combine squash, onion, egg, salt, and pepper. Mix well. Stir in flour, coating vegetables. In skillet, heat ½ inch oil over medium-high heat. Drop batter by tablespoon into oil. Cook on each side until golden brown. Drain on paper towels.

Denise McGuire

*Don't let the fancy name fool you. There's a
down-home goodness to these tasty treats.*

The Amish General Store

To walk into an Amish general store is to step back in time. Nearly every Amish community offers tourists and locals alike a quaint shopping experience, a place to taste local cuisines and purchase gifts for loved ones. Whether you're looking for furniture for your home, handcrafted wooden toys for the kids, a colorful quilt for Mom, gardening tools for Dad, or handcrafted soap for Grandma, you will find it here. The Amish know just what to offer to draw folks in.

In the mood to sample local cheeses? You will find them in abundance, along with other local products like fresh cheese curd, honey, and summer sausage. If that's not enough to win you over, then the smell of smoked bacon will surely tempt your senses.

And speaking of temptation, who can say no to homemade baked goods? Most Amish stores sell a plethora of sweet treats—breads, cinnamon rolls, whoopie pies, shoofly pies, fried pies, and cookies, just to name a few.

Hoping to take some of the sweets home with you? Head over to the jams and jellies aisle, where the abundance of flavors will tempt you once again. Or choose from other aisles of canned goods from apple butter and spiced peaches to pickled beets and chow chow. You can even take home a jar of peanut butter fluff, guaranteed to make the kids happy.

If you're looking for candy, you've come to the right place. You'll find buckeyes, cashew brittle, and a wide variety of fudges that will leave your mouth watering.

Want to grab a bite to eat before you leave? Head to the lunch counter to purchase an Amish sauerkraut sandwich. Why not pair it with a bowl of corn chowder while you're at it? And don't forget to enjoy a slice of hot bread, lathered in creamy local butter.

One piece of advice before you rush out the door: Things move at a slower pace in the Amish country. Take your time. Enjoy the experience. There will be plenty of opportunity to rush home later. For now, shake a hand or two. Say hello to the locals. And, as you head out to your car, wave to the fellow in the buggy as he plods on his way.

RECIPES FOR SNACKS, DIPS, AND SPICES

Let not him that eateth despise him that eateth not; and let not him which eateth not judge him that eateth: for God hath received him.

ROMANS 14:3

GREEN BEAN CHIPS

5 pounds fresh green beans, blanched	4 teaspoons salt
1/3 cup oil	1/4 cup nutritional yeast

Place green beans in large bowl. Pour oil on top. Sprinkle seasonings on top of coated beans and stir well. Dehydrate by putting beans on lined baking sheet in oven on its lowest setting for 6 to 8 hours, until crisp. Toss every hour. Store in airtight container.

Ellen Blackburn
A healthy snack for on the go.

SAUSAGE BALLS

1 pound ground sausage	10 ounces shredded cheddar cheese
3 cups biscuit mix (like Bisquick)	

Cook sausage. Drain. Add biscuit mix and cheese. Form into balls. Bake at 350 degrees about 25 minutes.

Kevin Cooper
Kevin enjoys helping in the kitchen when his family rolls and bakes these delights.

CREAM CHEESE DIP

1 (8 ounce) package cream cheese, softened	Garlic salt to taste
2 tablespoons Miracle Whip or mayonnaise	1/2 cup diced onion
	1 dash Worcestershire sauce

Mix cream cheese and Miracle Whip. Sprinkle in garlic salt, then add onion and Worcestershire sauce. Mix until creamy. Serve with your favorite chips, snack crackers, or veggies.

Denise McGuire
Even her finicky daughter, Kassidy, likes this cheesey dip.

Soft Pretzels

3 tablespoons yeast
2½ cups lukewarm water
¾ cup brown sugar
1 teaspoon salt

7 to 8 cups flour
2 tablespoons baking soda
1 cup water
Melted butter

Dissolve yeast in lukewarm water; add sugar and salt. Knead in flour. Allow to rise. Punch down once, then take pieces and roll out, forming desired pretzel shapes. Dissolve baking soda in 1 cup water. Dip pretzels in soda water. Let rise on baking sheet, then bake at 400 to 450 degrees for about eight minutes or until brown. Brush with butter.

VERA MAST, *Kalona, IA*

Cheese Ball

2 (8 ounce) packages cream cheese
8 ounces cheddar cheese, finely
   shredded
1 tablespoon Worcestershire sauce
1 tablespoon minced onion

1 teaspoon onion salt
1 teaspoon seasoned salt
½ cup chopped nuts
1 tablespoon dried parsley

Mix cream cheese, cheddar cheese, Worcestershire sauce, onion, and salts. Form into ball and roll in mixture of nuts and parsley.

Fran Nissley, Campbellsville, KY

Taco Dip

2 (8 ounce) packages cream cheese,
   softened
1 pound ground beef
½ medium onion

1 envelope taco seasoning
½ cup water
1 (8 ounce) bottle taco sauce
1 cup cheddar cheese

Spray oil on a 2-quart baking dish. Spread cream cheese on bottom. Fry ground beef and onion; coat in dry seasoning. Stir in water and cook until thick. Sprinkle meat mixture on the cream cheese and top with taco sauce then cheddar cheese. Bake at 375 degrees for 20 minutes until bubbly and melted.

Allie Barrett
A great appetizer to take to parties
from a woman who loves nachos.

Vegetable Dip

1 cup sour cream or plain yogurt
1 cup mayonnaise
1½ tablespoons minced onion or
   onion flakes

1½ tablespoons parsley
1½ teaspoons dill
1 teaspoon seasoned salt

Mix together all ingredients and chill. Serve with a platter of your favorite fresh vegetables.

Trent Cooper
Trent doesn't do much cooking, but this dip is
easy to whip up with his two children.

Mexi Corn Salsa

1 (15 ounce) can whole kernel corn, drained
1 (15 ounce) can black beans, rinsed and drained
1 large tomato, diced
¾ cup diced red bell pepper
½ cup diced green bell pepper
½ cup diced onion
½ cup Italian salad dressing
¼ cup minced fresh cilantro
2 tablespoons minced fresh parsley
½ teaspoon garlic powder

Combine all veggies in a bowl. Mix remaining ingredients and stir into veggies. Refrigerate several hours for flavors to blend. Serve with your choice of corn or tortilla chips.

KATHRYN TROYER, *Rutherford, TN*

Soft Spread Cheese

1 gallon skim milk
1 tablespoon citric acid
¼ cup cold water
1 teaspoon baking soda
1¼ teaspoons salt
¾ cup cream or milk
¼ cup butter (optional)

Heat milk to 140 degrees. Dissolve citric acid in water. Add to milk. Stir until milk separates and curds form. Curds can be all in one mass or they may separate into small fine lumps. Drain curds through cheesecloth for about 10 minutes. Dump curds into medium-sized kettle. Add baking soda, salt, cream, and butter. Heat on low heat and stir briskly until lumps are dissolved. When cheese is soft and smooth, put cheese into containers and cool. Delicious on bread or crackers! Cheese can be frozen. Note: More or less cream can be used depending on how thick or thin you want your cheese.

MRS. THOMAS BEACHY, *Liberty, KY*

SPINACH DIP

1 (10 ounce) package frozen chopped
   spinach
1½ cups sour cream
1 cup mayonnaise or Miracle Whip

1 package Knorr vegetable soup mix
1 (8 ounce) can chopped water
   chestnuts
3 green onions, chopped

Thaw spinach, place in towel, and squeeze until dry. Mix all other ingredients, blending well, then add spinach. Refrigerate 2 hours and stir. Serve with chips or crackers or hollow out a round loaf of bread and fill with dip.

Nichole Smith

*Nichole is happy to see her siblings will eat
something green when it comes to this dip.*

Allspice

½ teaspoon cinnamon   ¼ teaspoon nutmeg
¼ teaspoon cloves

Combine all ingredients in jar and store alongside your other spices.

Jerky Marinade

1½ teaspoons coarse pepper   1 tablespoon onion powder
2 tablespoons liquid smoke   ¼ cup soy sauce
1 tablespoon salt   ¼ cup Worcestershire sauce
½ teaspoon garlic powder

Combine all ingredients and stir. Cut meat of your choice into ¼-to ⅜-inch strips.
Marinate in mixture for 24 hours. Thread onto toothpicks and hang in oven on
low heat with door cracked for 8 to 10 hours.

Bill Mason/Editor

*Bill is excited to share the recipe for this
marinade, which he uses on all his deer jerky.*

Steak Marinade

½ cup olive oil   1 tablespoon rosemary
2 green onions, chopped   1 tablespoon vinegar
2 cloves garlic, minced   1 teaspoon Dijon mustard
1 tablespoon basil   1 teaspoon salt
1 tablespoon thyme   1 teaspoon pepper

Mix all ingredients. Pour over 4 to 5 pounds of steak and marinate for 1 to 2
days. Grill.

Susie R. Gingerich, *Kimbolton, OH*

Amish Children in the Kitchen

Amish children are raised with a strong work ethic and are taught to be productive members of their community. From the time they are very young, these little ones are given daily chores that include making their beds, sweeping floors, pulling weeds in the garden, and tending the animals. All this, in addition to going to school.

Amish children are also at home in the kitchen. They are taught to set the table before meals and clear their spots afterward. These youngsters are also skilled at helping in other ways, like gathering eggs from the henhouse. Daughters are taught to cook, to can, and to keep things tidy. In short, they're learning how to one day be productive mothers, capable of handling the daily grind in their own kitchen.

How does an Amish child glean information that will guide her to be a good cook? She listens in as her mother teaches a friend how to make Friendship Bread. She pays close attention as the local women gather to share recipes. She helps measure flour for Mother's yummy raisin cookies. She sets the table at mealtime, keenly aware of the foods that will be served. In short, she's already excited about cooking, even at a young age.

Just like all children, Amish youngsters love to try new things in the kitchen. Their culinary masterpieces might include apples with marshmallow fluff or buckeyes. You might find them helping Mother with a Lazy Daisy cake or a shoofly pie. You might even peek in as they mix and measure ingredients on their own, with no assistance from a grown-up.

Amish kids love putting together fun meals and snacks that everyone in the family will enjoy. Basically, they like to experiment. And with so many fresh ingredients surrounding them, there are plenty of opportunities. Whether they know it or not, these youngsters are carrying on the traditions of their mothers, grandmothers, and even great-grandmothers. What an amazing legacy, and what a wonderful way to keep the heart of the Amish kitchen alive.

RECIPES FOR CHILDREN

*My son, hear the instruction of
thy father, and forsake not the law
of thy mother: for they shall be an
ornament of grace unto thy head,
and chains about thy neck.*

PROVERBS 1:8–9

Baby's First Foods

APPLESAUCE (introduce at 6 to 8 months of age)

Apples (Gala, Rome, etc.)

Start by washing and peeling apples. Core and slice into chunks. Place pieces in pan and barely cover with water. Boil until apples are tender; drain and reserve juice. Mash apples by hand or in blender/food processor. If necessary, add reserved juice until you reach desired consistency. If you prefer, add a bit of homemade rice cereal or oatmeal to applesauce to thicken.

Kendra Perkins
According to Kendra, every new mom
needs to give homemade baby foods a try.
Why not start with this simple recipe?

CARROTS (introduce at 6 to 8 months of age)

2 large carrots, peeled and chopped
into small chunks

Cover carrots in water and boil until tender (15 to 20 minutes). Remove carrots from water and place in blender/food processor. You can use potato masher to mash, but remove all lumps. Add reserved water to achieve desired consistency.

PEAS (introduce at 6 to 8 months of age)

Fresh green peas

Purchase fresh peas that have a bright color. Open pods and scrape peas from their pods. Steam or boil peas in small amount of water. (Some mothers prefer to use homemade vegetable or chicken/beef broth.) Drain and reserve leftover water. Puree (by hand or in blender/food processor). Add reserved water to achieve desired consistency.

Oatmeal Cereal (introduce at 6 to 8 months of age)

½ cup old-fashioned oats

1½ cups water

Breast milk or baby's formula

Grind oats in blender or food processor. Bring water to a rapid boil in saucepan. Add ground oats and stir continually. Allow to simmer on low-medium heat for 10 minutes. Use whisk to keep mixture moving. Cool and mix with breast milk or baby's formula until desired consistency. If your baby is ready for fruits, mix in a bit of applesauce. Serve warm.

Rice Cereal (introduce at 6 to 8 months of age)

2 cups water
½ cup rice powder (brown rice ground
   in blender or food processor)

Breast milk or baby's formula

Bring water to a rapid boil in saucepan. Add rice powder and stir continually. Allow to simmer on medium-low heat for 10 minutes. Use whisk to keep mixture moving. Cool and mix with breast milk or baby's formula until desired consistency. If your baby is ready for fruits, mix in a bit of applesauce. Serve warm.

Kendra Perkins

Baby fussy at night? Perhaps it's time to start feeding him rice cereal. This recipe is the best, according to Kendra.

Squash (introduce at 6 to 8 months of age)

Butternut squash

Start by cutting squash in half lengthwise. Scoop out seeds and place squash facedown in oblong baking dish. Add a couple of inches of water. Bake at 400 degrees for about 40 minutes. The skin will pucker. Remove from oven and scoop out the "meat" of the squash, placing it into food processor or blender. (This can be done by hand with potato masher, but make sure you work out all lumps.) Add a bit of water to thin out puree.

Sweet Potato Puree (introduce at 6 to 8 months of age)

1 large sweet potato, diced

Cover sweet potato in water and boil until tender (about 15 minutes). Remove potato from water and place in blender/food processor. You can use potato masher to mash, but remove all lumps. Add reserved water to achieve desired consistency.

Kids' Favorites

Apple Rings with Peanut Butter

Peanut butter
1 apple, cored and sliced

Raisins
Pecans or walnuts, chopped

Spread peanut butter over apple slices and then top with raisins and nuts of your choice.

Randy and Marsha Olsen
The siblings love this tasty snack Heidi helps them make when they're hungry.

Buckeyes

1 pound creamy peanut butter
1½ pounds powdered sugar
1 cup butter or margarine, softened

1 (12 ounce) package chocolate chips
½ stick paraffin

Mix peanut butter and powdered sugar to piecrust consistency, then blend in butter. Roll into balls and chill thoroughly. Melt together chocolate chips and paraffin. Dip balls into chocolate and let dry.

CINDY MAST, *Danville, OH*

Yogurt Parfait

2 quarts vanilla or strawberry yogurt
4 ounces whipped topping

Granola
2 to 3 kinds of fresh chopped fruit

Mix yogurt and whipped topping. In tall glasses, place granola in the bottom, then a thick layer of yogurt. Add layers of fruit, yogurt, fruit. Top with granola.

LUELLA MILLER, *Shreve, OH*

CHOCOLATE-COVERED FROZEN BANANAS

Chocolate chips

Bananas

Skewers

Sprinkles

Melt chocolate chips in microwave. Stir until smooth. Peel bananas and cut in half. Stick skewers into flattened (cut off) end of each banana and coat with chocolate. While chocolate is still warm, add colorful sprinkles. Place in freezer-safe bag and chill in freezer for 30 minutes. Enjoy!

Debbie Cooper

Debbie thinks the best way to eat bananas is frozen in chocolate.

FRESH FRUIT SALAD

6 peaches, peeled, pitted, and
   chopped

1 pound fresh strawberries, rinsed,
   hulled, and sliced

½ pound seedless green grapes

½ pound seedless red grapes

3 bananas, peeled and sliced

Juice of one lime

½ cup pineapple juice

1 teaspoon ground ginger

In large serving bowl, combine cut up fruit and toss gently. In smaller bowl, whisk together lime and pineapple juices with ginger to make light dressing. Pour dressing mixture over fruit and toss gently to combine. Cover and chill fruit for 30 minutes or so before serving.

Heidi Trozer

Dump Cake

1 large can peaches in syrup (or canned fruit of your choice)
1 box white cake mix

1½ sticks butter
Whipped cream

Put peaches in 9x13-inch baking dish. Sprinkle cake mix over top of fruit. Slice butter into tablespoons and distribute evenly over surface of cake mix. Bake at 350 degrees for 45 minutes to 1 hour, until top is brown and bubbly. Serve with whipped cream.

Jeremy Keller

This is a recipe that even a young boy like Jeremy can make.

Egg Salad Sandwiches

3 hard-boiled eggs, peeled and chopped
⅛ cup mayonnaise (or more if mixture is too dry)
¼ teaspoon vinegar

⅛ teaspoon salt
⅛ teaspoon celery salt
1½ teaspoon yellow mustard
1½ teaspoon sugar
⅛ teaspoon onion salt

In medium-sized bowl, mix chopped eggs with mayonnaise and other ingredients, stirring well. Serve on bed of lettuce or make sandwich using fresh bread. A leaf of lettuce, pickles, or sliced olives may be added to the sandwich.

Heidi Troyer

Fruit Kebabs

Strawberries
Bananas
Blueberries

Large marshmallows
Skewers

Skewer fruit, alternating colors. Top off with marshmallow and enjoy.

Kassidy McGuire

This is Kassidy's favorite way to eat fruit.

Macaroni and Cheese

Small bag of pasta (in your choice of shape, approximately 16 ounces)

1 cup cubed Velveeta cheese

¼ cup milk

¼ cup butter

Salt and pepper to taste

Boil pasta until tender. Drain, rinse, and set aside. In small saucepan, combine remaining ingredients. Warm until cheese is melted and then add pasta. Stir until thickened and remove from heat.

Marsha Olsen

Marsha loves it when Heidi fixes macaroni and cheese.

Marshmallow Fluff for Apples

1 cup water

2 to 3 tablespoons molasses

2 cups creamy peanut butter

1 pint marshmallow cream

Bring water and molasses to a boil in large saucepan; remove from heat. Stir in peanut butter and marshmallow cream. If too thin, add more peanut butter and marshmallow in equal increments. Keep in airtight container in refrigerator. Serve with sliced apples.

Becky Blackburn

Becky loves peanut butter and this treat is one of her favorites.

Purple Cow

2 to 3 scoops vanilla ice cream or frozen yogurt

8 ounces grape juice

Scoop ice cream into glass then add grape juice. Enjoy!

Debbie Cooper

Debbie's mother makes this for her children as a fun and tasty drink.

Honey Granola Bars

3 cups quick oats
2 cups old-fashioned oats
1 cup coconut
1¼ cups Rice Krispies
½ cup sunflower seeds
1 cup nuts
¼ cup olive oil

1 cup butter, melted
1 cup natural peanut butter
¾ cup honey
2½ teaspoons vanilla
½ teaspoon salt
2 cups chocolate chips (optional)

Mix first six ingredients, then coat with olive oil. In bowl, combine butter, peanut butter, honey, vanilla, and salt. Pour over first mixture and mix well. Stir in chocolate chips. Press mixture into jelly roll pan. Press hard so bars won't be crumbly. Bake at 375 degrees for 20 minutes or until golden. Store in refrigerator.

Jolene Bontrager, *Topeka, IN*

Mini Corn Dogs

1⅓ cup white flour
⅓ cup cornmeal
1 tablespoon baking powder
1 teaspoon salt
1 tablespoon shortening

3 tablespoons butter, softened
¾ cup milk
1 package of hot dogs (each hot dog cut in half)

In medium size bowl, mix dry ingredients with shortening, butter, and milk. Using rolling pin, roll out dough on greased cutting board or mat. Cut circles from dough. A wide-mouth canning jar lid works fine for this. Place ½ of hot dog on each circle. Bring the sides of the dough up and pinch in the center. Place on greased cookie sheet and bake at 350 degrees for 12 to 15 minutes.

Heidi Troyer

Toasted Cheese Sandwich

2 slices bread
Butter

1 to 2 slices cheese

Butter one side of each slice of bread. Heat skillet and lay a buttered side down in the pan. Place cheese on bread. Cover with second slice of bread with butter facing up. Cover with lid for 2 minutes or until bread is lightly browned. Turn sandwich over and cook 2 more minutes until lightly browned. Serve.

Nichole Smith
This was one of the first things Nichole learned to make alongside her mom.

Peanut Butter Dogs

Peanut butter
Sliced bread

Bananas

Spread peanut butter on slice of bread, then peel banana and lay it across peanut butter, just as you would place a hot dog. Fold bread and enjoy.

Jeremy Keller
Jeremy has found a new way to eat bananas.

Pizza Pretzels

1 tablespoon sour cream-and-onion
  powder
2 tablespoons cheddar cheese powder

1 teaspoon pizza seasoning
1 pound pretzels
¾ cup oil

In large bowl, blend seasonings. Toss in pretzels. Coat with oil and stir to mix. Let stand for several minutes. Bake at 350 degrees for 15 minutes.

AMANDA HERSHBERGER, *Apple Creek, OH*

Vinegar Taffy

2 cups sugar	⅛ teaspoon cream of tartar
½ cup vinegar	1 pinch salt
2 tablespoons butter	Butter

In large saucepan over medium heat, combine sugar, vinegar, butter, cream of tartar, and salt. Heat, stirring occasionally, until sugar is melted. Stop stirring when mixture comes to a boil. Cook until mixture reaches 250 to 265 degrees, or until small amount of syrup dropped into cold water forms firm ball. Remove from heat and pour into buttered dish. Butter hands and pull taffy by stretching out into a rope. Fold it over and repeat until taffy turns white and becomes too stiff to pull. Cut into 1-inch pieces with buttered kitchen shears. Wrap taffy pieces in waxed paper and store in airtight container.

Eli Miller
*Eli recalls the many fun times he had with family
and friends when his wife prepared this recipe.*

Pudding over Ice Cream

1 small package chocolate or butterscotch pudding	2 cups milk
	Vanilla ice cream

Cook pudding mix in milk according to directions on box. Cool briefly. Serve warm over ice cream.

Peggy Ann Kimball
*Peggy Ann found something so simple she
can make that the whole family loves.*

Sticks and Stones

4 cups Kix cereal
2 cups pretzel sticks
⅓ cup melted butter

½ teaspoon Worcestershire sauce
2 cups raisins

Mix cereal and pretzels together. Mix butter and Worcestershire sauce. Pour over cereal. Bake at 300 degrees for 25 minutes. Stir in raisins.

Katie Zook, *Apple Creek, OH*

Puppy Chow

¼ cup butter
1 cup chocolate chips
½ cup peanut butter

9 cups Chex cereal
Powdered sugar

Melt butter, chocolate chips, and peanut butter. Pour over cereal and stir to coat. Sprinkle with powdered sugar to coat. Spread out to cool and dry. Store in sealed container.

Ada Mast, *Kalona, IA*

Chicken Nuggets

1 cup bread crumbs (or cracker meal)
1 egg
1 tablespoon water

1 cup flour
Salt and pepper to taste
Boneless, skinless chicken breasts

Put bread crumbs on rimmed plate and set aside. Beat egg with water in small bowl and set aside. Add flour and seasoning to plastic bag and set aside. Cube chicken breasts and place in bag with flour. Shake. Remove piece by piece and coat with egg, then coat in bread crumbs. Place on baking sheet and bake at 350 degrees for 12 minutes (flipping at the halfway point) until chicken is golden brown and cooked through.

Kevin Cooper
Chicken nuggets are one of his favorite foods.

Index

Index of Contributors

Index of Recipes by Section

———— ❦ ————

Recipes for Breakfast Foods 49

Recipes for Desserts. 63

CAKES AND BROWNIES

CANDY

BARS AND COOKIES

PIES

Miscellaneous Recipes 145

CANINE TREATS

HEALTH

HOUSEHOLD

Recipes for Salads and Sides 157

Index by Key Ingredient

Books by Wanda E. Brunstetter

KENTUCKY BROTHERS SERIES
The Journey
The Healing
The Struggle

INDIANA COUSINS SERIES
A Cousin's Promise
A Cousin's Prayer
A Cousin's Challenge

BRIDES OF LEHIGH CANAL SERIES
Kelly's Chance
Betsy's Return
Sarah's Choice

DAUGHTERS OF LANCASTER COUNTY
SERIES
The Storekeeper's Daughter
The Quilter's Daughter
The Bishop's Daughter

BRIDES OF LANCASTER COUNTY
SERIES
A Merry Heart
Looking for a Miracle
Plain and Fancy
The Hope Chest

SISTERS OF HOLMES COUNTY SERIES
A Sister's Secret
A Sister's Test
A Sister's Hope

PRAIRIE STATE FRIENDS SERIES
The Decision
The Gift
The Restoration

BRIDES OF WEBSTER COUNTY SERIES
Going Home
On Her Own
Dear to Me
Allison's Journey

THE HALF-STITCHED AMISH
QUILTING CLUB SERIES
The Half-Stitched Amish Quilting Club
The Tattered Quilt
The Healing Quilt

AMISH COOKING CLASS SERIES
The Seekers
The Blessing
The Celebration

NONFICTION
The Simple Life
A Celebration of the Simple Life
*Wanda E. Brunstetter's Amish Friends
Cookbook*
*Wanda E. Brunstetter's Amish Friends
Cookbook, Vol. 2*
*Wanda E. Brunstetter's Amish Friends
Christmas Cookbook*
*Wanda E. Brunstetter's Amish Friends
Harvest Cookbook*

CHILDREN'S BOOKS
Rachel Yoder—Always Trouble Some-
where Series (8 books)
The Wisdom of Solomon Lapp
Double Trouble Book 1: What a Pair!

STAND ALONE NOVELS
The Lopsided Christmas Cake
The Farmer's Market Mishap
The Hawaiian Quilt
The Hawaiian Discovery
White Christmas Pie
Lydia's Charm
Woman of Courage

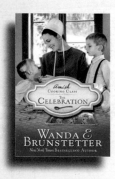